Taste of Home
salads & sandwiches

207 Fresh, New Takes on a Classic Combination!

Whether they are for lunch, a light supper, a potluck or snack, salads and sandwiches provide tasty alternatives to standard fare. Fresh, packed with flavor and simple to toss together, the 207 no-fuss, enticing creations in **Taste of Home Salads & Sandwiches** will have you thinking outside the "lunch box" with delicious ideas for every occasion—and for every meal of the day.

Organized into eight hearty chapters, this pleasing assortment features Prize Winners; Hot Sandwiches; Cold Sandwiches; Green Salads; Potatoes, Pasta & More; Breakfast on the Go; Wraps, Pitas & Specialty Sandwiches; and Crowd Pleasers.

One bite of the satisfying salads in this collection, and you'll no longer think of them as "rabbit food." From the can't-fail classics such as Caesar, Cobb and Waldorf to new taste twists like Watermelon Spinach Salad (p. 55), Cucumber Potato Salad (p. 66) and Spicy Ravioli Salad (p. 15), these appealing combinations are raising the salad bar. You will even enjoy a selection of colorful, fruity salads and sweet gelatin delights.

When it comes to sandwiches, get ready to sink your teeth into everything from timeless standbys like Hearty Ham Sandwiches (p. 41) and Make-Ahead Sloppy Joes (p. 107) to future favorites like Barbecued Chicken Salad Sandwiches (p. 36) and Curry Cheddar Grill (p. 28). Stacked high or open-faced, the hoagies, subs, melts and clubs in this book boast examples of superior sandwichery that will have your taste buds tingling.

With choices ranging from cold to grilled sandwiches, wraps to pitas, entree salads to pasta tosses and everything in between, this refreshing, generous mix will have you saying "goodbye" to the deli and "hello" to **Taste of Home Salads & Sandwiches**.

Taste of Home Reader's digest

President and
Chief Executive Officer: Mary G. Berner
President, Food & Entertaining: Suzanne M. Grimes
Editor in Chief: Catherine Cassidy
Vice President,
Executive Editor/Books: Heidi Reuter Lloyd
Creative Director: Ardyth Cope
Editor: Sara Lancaster
Senior Editor/Books: Mark Hagen
Art Director: Gretchen Trautman
Content Production Supervisor: Julie Wagner
Layout Designers: Catherine Fletcher
Kathy Crawford
Proofreader: Linne Bruskewitz
Indexer: Jean Steiner
Editorial Assistant: Barb Czysz

Food Director: Diane Werner RD
Test Kitchen Manager: Karen Scales
Recipe Editors: Sue A. Jurack (Senior)
Mary King
Christine Rukavena
Recipe Asset System Manager: Coleen Martin
Test Kitchen Assistant: Rita Krajcir

Studio Photographers: Rob Hagen (Senior)
Dan Roberts
Jim Wieland
Lori Foy
Senior Food Stylist: Sarah Thompson
Food Stylist Assistants: Kaitlyn Basasie
Alynna Malson
Set Stylists: Jennifer Bradley Vent (Senior)
Dee Dee Jacq
Photo Studio Coordinator: Kathleen Swaney

Cover Photography: Rob Hagen (Photographer)
Jim Rude (Food Stylist)
Grace Natoli-Sheldon (Set Stylist)

©2008 Reiman Media Group, Inc.
5400 S. 60th Street, Greendale WI 53129

International Standard Book Number (10): 0-89821-687-7
International Standard Book Number (13): 978-0-89821-687-5
Library of Congress Control Number: 2007938916

Pictured on front cover: Hot Colby Ham Sandwiches (p. 23)
Roasted Potato Salad (p. 102)

Pictured on back cover: Submarine Sandwich Salad (p. 50)

salads & sandwiches

Taste of Home Salads & Sandwiches makes a great gift for those who like to eat fresh. To order additional copies, specify item number 37551 and send $15.99 (plus $4.99 shipping/processing for one book, $5.99 for two or more) to: Shop Taste of Home, Suite 144, P.O. Box 26820, Lehigh Valley, PA 18002-6820. To order **Taste of Home Salads & Sandwiches** by credit card, call toll-free 1-800/880-3012.

1 prize winners

Declared the best-of-the-best, this mouth-watering assortment is jam-packed with crisp green salads, pasta medleys, hearty sandwiches, stacked hoagies and other prize-winning favorites. And because every recipe is a proud *Taste of Home* contest winner, they're guaranteed to stand out.

page 13

page 9

page 11

Cobb Salad Wraps

Cobb Salad Wraps

Lynn Van Wagenen ☀ LAKE CITY, UTAH

A homemade dressing lightens up these refreshing tortilla wraps. The avocado, bacon, blue cheese and tomato deliver the flavors I enjoy most while keeping me on my healthy eating plan.

USES LESS FAT, SUGAR OR SALT. INCLUDES NUTRITION FACTS.

1/2	pound boneless skinless chicken breasts, cooked and shredded
1/2	cup chopped avocado
4	bacon strips, cooked and crumbled
1	celery rib, thinly sliced
1	green onion, sliced
2	tablespoons chopped ripe olives
2	tablespoons crumbled blue cheese
2	tablespoons lemon juice
1	tablespoon honey
1-1/2	teaspoons Dijon mustard
1	garlic clove, minced
1/4	teaspoon dill weed
1/4	teaspoon salt
1/8	teaspoon pepper
1	tablespoon olive oil
4	romaine leaves, torn
4	whole wheat tortilla (8 inches), warmed
1	medium tomato, chopped

In a small bowl, combine the chicken, avocado, bacon, celery, onion, olives and cheese. In another small bowl, combine the lemon juice, honey, mustard, garlic, dill weed, salt and pepper. Whisk in the oil. Pour over the chicken mixture; toss to coat. Place romaine on each tortilla; top with 2/3 cup chicken mixture. Sprinkle with tomatoes; roll up. **Yield: 4 servings.**

NUTRITION FACTS: 1 wrap equals 324 calories, 14 g fat (4 g saturated fat), 57 mg cholesterol, 608 mg sodium, 30 g carbohydrate, 4 g fiber, 24 g protein.

Cashew Turkey Pasta Salad

Karen Wyffels ☀ LINO LAKES, MINNESOTA

Cashews add a nice crunch to this grilled turkey and spiral pasta combo. I first tasted this salad at a baby shower and asked the hostess for her recipe. Since then, I have served the dish for many occasions.

2	bone-in turkey breast halves, skin removed
3	cups uncooked tricolor spiral pasta
2	celery ribs, diced
6	green onions, chopped
1/2	cup diced green pepper
1-1/2	cups mayonnaise
3/4	cup packed brown sugar
1	tablespoon cider vinegar
1-1/2	teaspoons salt
1-1/2	teaspoons lemon juice
2	cups salted cashew halves

Grill turkey, covered, over medium heat for 25-30 minutes on each side or until juices run clear. Cool slightly. Cover turkey and refrigerate until cool. Meanwhile, cook pasta according to package directions; drain and rinse in cold water.

Chop turkey; place in a large bowl. Add the pasta, celery, onions and green pepper. In a small bowl, combine the mayonnaise, brown sugar, vinegar, salt and lemon juice; pour over pasta mixture and toss to coat. Cover and refrigerate pasta salad for at least 2 hours. Just before serving, stir in cashews. **Yield: 12 servings.**

Cashew Turkey Pasta Salad

Bacon-Tomato Bagel Melts

Chicken Chopped Salad

Diane Halferty ✳ CORPUS CHRISTI, TEXAS

Lime dressing gives lively flavor to this crunchy salad tossed with peaches, peppers and peanuts. The unusual combination is a great way to use up leftover chicken or turkey. Plus, it packs well for lunches or picnics.

2	cups chopped *or* torn mixed salad greens
2	cups chopped cooked chicken
1	cup chopped celery
1	can (15-1/4 ounces) peaches, drained and chopped
1	cup chopped sweet red *or* yellow pepper
1/3	cup limeade concentrate
1/4	cup vegetable oil
2	tablespoons white vinegar
2	to 3 tablespoons minced fresh cilantro
1-1/2	teaspoons minced fresh gingerroot
1/4	teaspoon salt
1/2	cup dry roasted peanuts

In a large salad bowl, combine the first five ingredients. In a jar with a tight-fitting lid, combine the limeade concentrate, oil, vinegar, cilantro, ginger and salt; shake well. Pour over salad and toss to coat. Sprinkle with peanuts. Serve immediately. **Yield: 6 servings.**

Bacon-Tomato Bagel Melts

Lindsay Orwig ✳ GRAND TERRACE, CALIFORNIA

My husband introduced me to this open-faced melt shortly after we got married, and it quickly became an all-time favorite. It's good made with plain or onion bagels.

2	bagels, split and toasted
8	tomato slices
8	cooked bacon strips
1	cup (4 ounces) shredded part-skim mozzarella cheese

Prepared ranch salad dressing

Place bagel halves cut side up on a baking sheet. Top each half with two tomato slices and two bacon strips. Sprinkle with cheese.

Broil 4-6 in. from the heat for 1-2 minutes or until cheese begins to brown. Serve with ranch dressing. **Yield: 4 sandwiches.**

Chicken Chopped Salad

tomato TIP

The best way to cut through the skin of a tomato is with a serrated, not straight-edged, knife. Cut a tomato vertically, from stem end to blossom end, for slices that will be less juicy and hold their shape better.

Flank Steak Spinach Salad

Freddie Johnson ✳ SAN ANTONIO, TEXAS

Moist, marinated steak, wild rice, almonds and fresh veggies blend together nicely in this colorful main-dish salad. A friend gave me the idea for this satisfying recipe, and with some tweaking, it has become a real favorite of ours.

4	beef flank steaks (about 1 pound *each*)
1	bottle (16 ounces) Italian salad dressing, *divided*
1-1/4	cups uncooked wild rice
2	packages (6 ounces *each*) fresh baby spinach
1/2	pound fresh mushrooms, sliced
1	large red onion, thinly sliced
1	pint grape tomatoes, halved
1	package (2-1/2 ounces) slivered almonds, toasted

Place steaks in a gallon-size resealable plastic bag; add 3/4 cup salad dressing. Seal bag and turn to coat. Refrigerate steak overnight. Prepare the rice according to package directions. In a bowl, combine rice with 1/2 cup salad dressing. Cover and refrigerate rice overnight.

Drain and discard marinade from steaks. Grill steaks, uncovered, over medium heat for 6-8 minutes on each side or until meat reaches desired doneness (for medium-rare, a meat thermometer should read 145°; medium, 160°; well-done, 170°). Let stand for 10 minutes. Thinly slice steaks against the grain; cool to room temperature.

To serve, arrange spinach on a large platter. Top with the rice, mushrooms, onion, tomatoes and steak. Sprinkle with almonds; drizzle with remaining salad dressing. **Yield: 16 servings.**

Cheesy Chicken Subs

Flank Steak Spinach Salad

Cheesy Chicken Subs

Jane Hollar ✳ VILAS, NORTH CAROLINA

I've been part of the Food Services staff at Appalachian State University for 33 years. One summer we created this flavorful sub that combines slices of seasoned chicken, Swiss cheese and sauteed mushrooms and onions. Thousands of students have enjoyed them since then.

12	ounces boneless skinless chicken breasts, cut into strips
1	envelope Parmesan Italian *or* Caesar salad dressing mix
1	cup sliced fresh mushrooms
1/2	cup sliced red onion
1/4	cup olive oil
4	submarine buns, split and toasted
4	slices Swiss cheese

Place chicken in a bowl; sprinkle with salad dressing mix. In a skillet, saute mushrooms and onion in oil for 3 minutes. Add chicken; saute for 6 minutes or until chicken juices run clear.

Spoon mixture onto roll bottoms; top with cheese. Broil 4 in. from the heat for 4 minutes or until cheese is melted. Replace tops. **Yield: 4 servings.**

Catfish Po'boys

Mildred Sherrer ✳ ROANOKE, TEXAS

Here's a Southern favorite your family will love. A zesty cornmeal mixture coats catfish strips in these filling sandwiches.

2	tablespoons fat-free mayonnaise
1	tablespoon fat-free sour cream
1	tablespoon white wine vinegar
1	teaspoon sugar
2	cups broccoli coleslaw mix
1/4	cup cornmeal
2	teaspoons Cajun seasoning
1/2	teaspoon salt
1/8	teaspoon cayenne pepper
2	tablespoons fat-free milk
1	pound catfish fillets, cut into 2-1/2-inch strips
2	teaspoons olive oil
4	kaiser rolls, split

In a small bowl, whisk the mayonnaise, sour cream, vinegar and sugar until smooth. Add coleslaw mix; toss to coat. Set aside.

In a large resealable plastic bag, combine the cornmeal, Cajun seasoning, salt and cayenne. Place the milk in a shallow bowl. Dip a few pieces of fish at a time in milk, then place in bag; seal and shake to coat.

In a large nonstick skillet, cook catfish over medium heat in oil for 4-5 minutes on each side or until fish flakes easily with a fork and coating is golden brown. Spoon coleslaw onto rolls; top with catfish. **Yield: 4 servings.**

Apple Tuna Sandwiches

Ivy Eresmas ✳ DADE CITY, FLORIDA

My husband and his buddies love to pack these tasty sandwiches when they go on fishing trips. The tangy tuna salad gets fun flavor from sweet pickle relish and lots of crunch from apples, celery and walnuts. Best of all, they make a complete meal all by themselves.

USES LESS FAT, SUGAR OR SALT. INCLUDES NUTRITION FACTS.

1/3	cup fat-free mayonnaise
1/4	cup finely chopped celery
1/4	cup finely chopped walnuts
2	tablespoons finely chopped onion
1	tablespoon sweet pickle relish
1	teaspoon sugar

Apple Tuna Sandwiches

1/4	teaspoon salt
1	can (6 ounces) light water-packed tuna, drained
1/2	cup chopped red apple
6	slices reduced-calorie bread, toasted
6	lettuce leaves

In a large bowl, combine the first seven ingredients; stir in tuna and apple. Spread 1/2 cup tuna mixture on three slices of bread. Top with lettuce and remaining bread. **Yield: 3 servings.**

NUTRITION FACTS: 1/2 cup (calculated without bread) equals 201 calories, 9 g fat (0 saturated fat), 21 mg cholesterol, 237 mg sodium, 18 g carbohydrate, 3 g fiber, 12 g protein.

Bacon 'n' Egg Sandwiches

Ann Fuemmeler ✳ GLASGOW, MISSOURI

I came across this swift and delicious combo when I was digging in my mom's recipe box. The crisp bacon, hard-cooked eggs and green onions make these special bites look impressive, when they're really a snap to assemble.

1/2	cup sour cream
8	slices bread
4	green onions, chopped
4	slices process American cheese
2	hard-cooked eggs, cut into 1/4-inch slices
8	bacon strips, cooked and drained
1/4	cup butter, softened

Spread sour cream on one side of four slices of bread. Top with onions, cheese, eggs and bacon. Top with the remaining bread. Butter outsides of sandwiches; cook in a large skillet over medium heat until golden brown on both sides. **Yield: 4 servings.**

Apple-Walnut Turkey Sandwiches

Apple-Walnut Turkey Sandwiches

Cathy Dobbins ✳ RIO RANCHO, NEW MEXICO

When you live where temperatures easily climb to 100° or more in the summer, you look for recipes that get you in and out of the kitchen in minutes. This luscious sandwich, with its cool Waldorf salad filling, is a breeze to prepare.

- 3/4   cup mayonnaise
- 1/4   cup chopped celery
- 1/4   cup raisins
- 1/4   cup chopped walnuts, toasted
- 1   medium tart apple, chopped

Lettuce leaves

- 8   slices sourdough bread
- 3/4   pound sliced deli turkey

In a large bowl, combine the mayonnaise, celery, raisins and walnuts. Stir in apple; set aside. Place lettuce on four slices of bread. Top with apple mixture, turkey and remaining bread. **Yield: 4 servings.**

Sesame Cucumber Salad

Linda Hodge ✳ KANNAPOLIS, NORTH CAROLINA

I learned to cook at an early age and have collected many recipes. Whenever I take this salad to a church supper, it's the first one to disappear.

- 8   cups thinly sliced cucumbers
- 1   tablespoon salt
- 2   green onions, sliced
- 1   garlic clove, minced
- 2   to 3 tablespoons soy sauce
- 2   tablespoons white vinegar
- 1   tablespoon vegetable oil
- 1   tablespoon sesame seeds, toasted
- 1/8   teaspoon cayenne pepper

Place cucumbers in a colander. Set the colander on a plate; sprinkle cucumbers with salt and toss. Let stand for 30 minutes. Rinse and drain well.

In a bowl, combine the onions, garlic, soy sauce, white vinegar, oil, sesame seeds and cayenne. Add cucumbers and toss to coat. Cover and refrigerate until serving. **Yield: 8-10 servings.**

Drop-in Salad

Kimber Archuleta ✳ EVANSTON, WYOMING

When my husband and I were invited to a barbecue, I threw together this broccoli salad. I tossed in whatever I had in the fridge, and the crunchy, colorful combination that resulted was a hit.

- 6   cups fresh broccoli florets
- 1-1/2   cups cubed cheddar cheese
- 1   large red apple, cubed
- 1   cup coarsely chopped pecans
- 1   small red onion, chopped
- 1/2   cup red wine vinaigrette *or* vinaigrette of your choice
- 1/2   teaspoon lemon juice

In a large salad bowl, combine the first five ingredients. Combine vinaigrette and lemon juice; drizzle over salad. Toss to coat. **Yield: 8-10 servings.**

Drop-in Salad

Oriental Pork Burgers

Oriental Pork Burgers

Deborah Messerly ✳ STEAMBOAT ROCK, IOWA

My home state of Iowa is a leader in pork production, and these grilled burgers are a truly delicious and nutritious way to use ground pork.

1	cup soft bread crumbs
1/3	cup finely chopped green onions
1/3	cup finely chopped green pepper
1	can (8 ounces) water chestnuts, drained and chopped
1	egg, lightly beaten
2	tablespoons soy sauce
1	garlic clove, minced
1	teaspoon salt
1/8	teaspoon ground ginger
2	pounds ground pork

SAUCE:

1	can (8 ounces) crushed pineapple, drained
2/3	cup ketchup
1/4	cup white vinegar
1/4	cup orange marmalade
2	tablespoons prepared mustard
8	hamburger buns, split and toasted

In a large bowl, combine the first nine ingredients. Crumble pork over mixture and mix well. Shape into eight patties. Cover and refrigerate for 1 hour.

Meanwhile, in a saucepan, combine the pineapple, ketchup, vinegar, marmalade and mustard. Cook and stir for 5 minutes or until the marmalade is melted. Remove from the heat; set aside.

Grill patties, covered, over medium heat for 4-6 minutes on each side or until meat is no longer pink. Spoon 1 tablespoon of sauce onto each burger during the last 2 minutes of grilling. Serve on buns with remaining sauce. **Yield: 8 servings.**

Tortellini Caesar Salad

Tammy Steenbock ✳ SEMBACH AIR BASE, GERMANY

A health-conscious friend, who suggested the dressing be prepared with low-fat or fat-free ingredients, served this salad at a baby shower. No matter how you prepare the creamy dressing, it has plenty of garlic flavor and coats the tortellini, romaine lettuce and croutons nicely.

USES LESS FAT, SUGAR OR SALT. INCLUDES NUTRITION FACT.

1	package (19 ounces) frozen cheese tortellini
1/2	cup mayonnaise
1/4	cup milk
1/4	cup plus 1/3 cup shredded Parmesan cheese, *divided*
2	tablespoons lemon juice
2	garlic cloves, minced
8	cups torn romaine
1	cup seasoned salad croutons

Halved cherry tomatoes, optional

Cook cheese tortellini according to package directions. Meanwhile, in a small bowl, combine the mayonnaise, milk, 1/4 cup Parmesan cheese, lemon juice and garlic.

Drain tortellini and rinse in cold water; transfer to a large bowl. Add romaine and remaining Parmesan. Just before serving, drizzle with dressing; toss to coat. Top with croutons and tomatoes if desired. **Yield: 10 servings.**

NUTRITION FACTS: 1 serving (prepared with fat-free mayonnaise and fat-free milk and without tomatoes) equals 144 calories, 4 g fat (0 saturated fat), 14 mg cholesterol, 318 mg sodium, 18 g carbohydrate, 1 g fiber, 8 g protein.

Tortellini Caesar Salad

Peppery Philly Steaks

Sweet-Sour Citrus Salad

Dorothy Swanson ✳ AFFTON, MISSOURI

The combination of fruit and garden-fresh vegetables tossed with a honey and poppy seed dressing makes this salad versatile enough to accompany any entree. My husband and I love it!

USES LESS FAT, SUGAR OR SALT. INCLUDES NUTRITION FACTS.

1	large pink grapefruit, peeled and sectioned
1	large navel orange, peeled and sectioned
1	tablespoon sugar
1	large sweet red pepper, julienned
1	small red onion, sliced and separated into rings
1/3	cup honey
1/4	cup cider vinegar
2	tablespoons poppy seeds
2	teaspoons grated onion
2	teaspoons lemon juice
1	teaspoon salt
1	teaspoon ground mustard
1/2	teaspoon grated lemon peel
4	cups torn salad greens
2	cups sliced fresh mushrooms

In a large bowl, combine the grapefruit and orange sections; sprinkle with sugar. Add red pepper and red onion. In a blender, combine the honey, vinegar, poppy seeds, grated onion, lemon juice, salt, mustard and lemon peel; cover and process until blended. Pour over fruit mixture and toss to coat.

In a large serving bowl, toss the salad greens, mushrooms and fruit mixture. **Yield: 6 servings.**

NUTRITION FACTS: 1 cup equals 132 calories, 2 g fat (0.55 g saturated fat), 0 cholesterol, 404 mg sodium, 30 g carbohydrate, 3 g fiber, 3 g protein.

Sweet-Sour Citrus Salad

Peppery Philly Steaks

Edie Fitch ✳ CLIFTON, ARIZONA

Since we love to cook and eat, my husband and I are always developing new recipes to enjoy. This is one we especially like to prepare when we have fresh peppers on hand.

1-1/2	pounds boneless sirloin steak, cut into 1/4-inch strips
1	medium green pepper, julienned
1	medium sweet red pepper, julienned
1	large onion, thinly sliced
3	tablespoons vegetable oil
2	tablespoons butter
5	to 6 French *or* Italian sandwich rolls, split
2	cans (4 ounces *each*) whole green chilies, drained and halved
5	to 6 slices Swiss cheese

In a large skillet, cook the steak, peppers and onion over medium heat in oil until meat is no longer pink. Spread butter on rolls; top with meat mixture, chilies and cheese. Wrap in heavy-duty foil.

Bake at 350° for 10-12 minutes or until heated through and cheese is melted. **Yield: 5-6 servings.**

Hearty Pasta Salad

Marcia Buchanan ✳ PHILADELPHIA, PENNSYLVANIA

When made with tricolor pasta, this is a colorful and tasty addition to any social gathering. It is delicious whether you prepare it using pastrami, turkey or roast beef.

2	cups uncooked spiral pasta
1	cup cooked cubed pastrami, turkey *or* roast beef

1/4 cup *each* chopped carrot, celery and onion

3/4 cup mayonnaise

1/4 cup grated Parmesan cheese

1/4 teaspoon salt

1/4 teaspoon pepper

1/4 teaspoon lemon juice

Cook pasta according to package directions; drain and rinse with cold water.

In a bowl, combine the pasta, pastrami, carrot, celery and onion. In another bowl, combine mayonnaise, Parmesan cheese, salt, pepper and lemon juice. Add to pasta mixture; toss to coat. Cover and refrigerate for 1 hour or until serving. **Yield: 4 servings.**

Cran-Apple Salad

Lucille Foster ✳ GRANT, NEBRASKa

This tart, ruby red salad goes so wonderfully with lots of different meals. With only four ingredients, it takes just minutes.

USES LESS FAT, SUGAR OR SALT. INCLUDES NUTRITION FACTS.

1 can (16 ounces) whole-berry cranberry sauce

1 medium unpeeled tart apple, diced

1 celery rib, thinly sliced

1/2 cup chopped walnuts

In a large salad bowl, combine the cranberry sauce, apple and celery. Cover salad and refrigerate until serving. Just before serving, stir in the chopped walnuts. **Yield: 4-6 servings.**

NUTRITION FACTS: 1 cup equals 183 calories, 6 g fat (trace saturated fat), 0 cholesterol, 22 mg sodium, 32 g carbohydrate, 2 g fiber, 3 g protein.

Cran-Apple Salad

Southwestern Pulled Pork

Southwestern Pulled Pork

Jill Hartung ✳ COLORADO SPRINGS, COLORADO

The best way to describe this tender pork recipe is "yummy!" Bottled barbecue sauce, canned green chilies and a few other kitchen staples make preparation fast and easy. We like to wrap the seasoned pork in flour tortillas.

2 cans (4 ounces *each*) chopped green chilies

1 can (8 ounces) tomato sauce

1 cup barbecue sauce

1 large sweet onion, thinly sliced

1/4 cup chili powder

1 teaspoon ground cumin

1 teaspoon dried oregano

1 boneless pork loin roast (2 to 2-1/2 pounds)

Flour tortillas

Sour cream, shredded lettuce and chopped tomatoes, optional

In a 3-qt. slow cooker, combine the chilies, tomato sauce, barbecue sauce, onion, chili powder, cumin and oregano. Cut pork roast in half; place on top of tomato sauce mixture. Cover and cook on low for 8-9 hours or until meat is tender.

Remove pork. When cool enough to handle, shred meat using two forks. Return meat to slow cooker and heat through. Spread on tortillas; top with sour cream, shredded lettuce and chopped tomatoes if desired; roll up. **Yield: 6-8 servings.**

Onion Beef Au Jus

Onion Beef Au Jus

Marilyn Brown ✳ WEST UNION, IOWA

Garlic, soy sauce and onion soup mix flavor the tender beef featured in these savory hot sandwiches served with a tasty rich broth for dipping. The seasoned meat makes delicious cold sandwiches, too.

1	boneless beef rump roast (4 pounds)
2	tablespoons vegetable oil
2	large sweet onions, cut into 1/4-inch slices
6	tablespoons butter, softened, *divided*
5	cups water
1/2	cup soy sauce
1	envelope onion soup mix
1	garlic clove, minced
1	teaspoon browning sauce, optional
1	loaf (1 pound) French bread
1	cup (4 ounces) shredded Swiss cheese

In a Dutch oven over medium-high heat, brown roast on all sides in oil; drain. In a large skillet, saute onions in 2 tablespoons of butter until tender. Add the water, soy sauce, soup mix, garlic and browning sauce if desired. Pour over roast. Cover and bake roast at 325° for 2-1/2 hours or until the meat is tender.

Let roast stand for 10 minutes before slicing. Return meat to pan juices. Slice French bread in half lengthwise; cut into 3-in. sections. Spread remaining butter over bread.

Place bread on baking sheet. Broil 4-6 in. from the heat for 2-3 minutes or until golden brown. Top with beef and onions; sprinkle with cheese. Broil 4-6 in. from the heat for 1-2 minutes or until cheese is melted. Serve with pan juices. **Yield: 12 servings.**

Cranberry Turkey Burgers

Barbara Lindauer ✳ NEW ATHENS, ILLINOIS

These turkey burgers are so good that you might give up traditional beef hamburgers altogether. The thick, grilled patties are topped with prepared cranberry sauce and served on toasted English muffins for a nice change of pace.

1	small tart apple, peeled and finely chopped
1	celery rib, chopped
1	small onion, chopped
1	teaspoon poultry seasoning
3/4	teaspoon salt
1/4	teaspoon pepper
1-1/4	pounds ground turkey
1/2	cup mayonnaise
6	English muffins, split and toasted
6	lettuce leaves
1	cup whole-berry cranberry sauce

In a large bowl, combine the first six ingredients. Crumble turkey over mixture and mix well. Shape into six patties. Coat grill rack with nonstick cooking spray before starting the grill. Grill patties, covered, over medium heat for 10 minutes on each side or until a meat thermometer reads 165°.

Spread mayonnaise over the muffin halves. Place lettuce, turkey burgers and cranberry sauce on muffin bottoms; replace tops. **Yield: 6 servings.**

Crabby Bagels

Connie Faulkner ✳ MOXEE, WASHINGTON

When my husband and I get tired of the peanut butter and jelly our daughter favors, we make this "grown-up" sandwich shared by a lady at church.

1	can (6 ounces) crabmeat, drained, flaked and cartilage removed
1/2	cup shredded cheddar cheese
1/4	cup finely chopped celery
1/4	cup sour cream
3/4	teaspoon Worcestershire sauce
1/4	teaspoon salt
4	onion bagels, split
1	package (3 ounces) cream cheese, softened
4	lettuce leaves

In a bowl, combine the first six ingredients. Toast bagels; spread with cream cheese. On the bottom

Cranberry Orange Vinaigrette

Spicy Ravioli Salad

Paula Marchesi ✳ LENHARTSVILLE, PENNSYLVANIA

You'll be sitting down to dinner in no time when you prepare this main-dish salad. A convenient combination of frozen ravioli and pantry staples is dressed with taco sauce for zesty results.

1 package (25 ounces) frozen beef, sausage *or* cheese ravioli
1 can (10 ounces) diced tomatoes and green chilies, undrained
1 can (8-3/4 ounces) whole kernel corn, drained
1 bottle (8 ounces) taco sauce
1 can (2-1/4 ounces) sliced ripe olives, drained
1 small cucumber, peeled, seeded and chopped
1 small red onion, sliced
2 garlic cloves, minced
1/4 teaspoon ground cumin
1/4 teaspoon salt
1/4 teaspoon pepper

Cook ravioli according to package directions. Meanwhile, in a large bowl, combine remaining ingredients. Drain ravioli and rinse with cold water; stir into tomato mixture. Cover and refrigerate for at least 2 hours. **Yield: 8-10 servings.**

of each bagel, place a lettuce leaf and 1/4 cup of crab mixture. Replace tops. **Yield: 4 servings.**

Cranberry Orange Vinaigrette

Toni Serpe ✳ DANIA, FLORIDA

I eat a lot of salad and this is one of my favorite dressings. Living in Florida, I like using orange products produced in our state.

1/4 cup cranberry juice concentrate
1/4 cup orange juice concentrate
1/4 cup red wine vinegar
1/4 cup olive oil
1 teaspoon Dijon mustard
1/2 teaspoon salt
1/2 teaspoon pepper
Torn salad greens
Sliced radishes and sweet yellow and orange peppers *or* vegetables of your choice

In a jar with a tight-fitting lid, combine the first seven ingredients; shake well. Serve dressing over the greens and vegetables. Store dressing in the refrigerator. **Yield: 1 cup.**

salad SUCCESS

To keep salad greens and cut vegetables fresh, put them in a plastic bag with a piece of paper towel. The paper towel will absorb any liquid so the produce lasts much longer.

Spicy Ravioli Salad

Shrimp Taco Salad

Layered Deli Loaf

Sarah Kraemer ✳ ROCKFORD, ILLINOIS

This recipe is special to me because it was handed down from my grandma. A tangy sauce, flavored with horseradish and Dijon mustard, sparks a hearty assortment of meats and cheeses. It feeds a crowd, so it's perfect for a party or potluck.

1/4	cup mayonnaise
2	tablespoons prepared horseradish, drained
1	tablespoon Dijon mustard
1	round loaf (1 pound) unsliced bread
2	tablespoons butter, softened
1/3	pound thinly sliced deli ham
1/3	pound sliced Monterey Jack cheese
1/3	pound thinly sliced deli turkey
1/3	pound sliced cheddar cheese
1/3	pound thinly sliced deli roast beef
1	medium tomato, sliced
1	large dill pickle, sliced lengthwise
1	small red onion, thinly sliced

Lettuce leaves

In a small bowl, combine the mayonnaise, horseradish and mustard. Cut bread in half. Carefully hollow out bottom and top of loaf, leaving 3/4-in. shell (discard removed bread or save for another use). Spread butter on cut sides of bread.

In the shell, layer ham, a third of the mayonnaise mixture, Monterey Jack cheese, turkey, a third of the mayonnaise mixture, cheddar cheese, roast beef, remaining mayonnaise mixture, tomato, pickle, onion and lettuce.

Replace top. Wrap tightly in plastic wrap; cover and refrigerate for at least 1 hour. **Yield: 8 servings.**

Shrimp Taco Salad

Ellen Morrell ✳ HAZLETON, PENNSYLVANIA

I created this entree salad to satisfy our family's love of shrimp. A convenient bag of salad greens cuts down on prep time, so I can have this meal ready in half an hour.

1	pound uncooked large shrimp, peeled and deveined
1	envelope taco seasoning, *divided*
1/2	cup plus 3 tablespoons olive oil, *divided*
1	small onion, finely chopped
3	tablespoons cider vinegar
2	tablespoons diced green *or* sweet red pepper
6	garlic cloves, minced
1/2	teaspoon ground coriander
1/4	teaspoon sugar
3	corn tortillas (6 inches), cut into 1/4-inch strips
1	package (8 ounces) ready-to-serve salad greens
1	medium tomato, chopped
1	can (8 ounces) black beans, rinsed and drained
2	cups (8 ounces) finely shredded Colby-Monterey Jack cheese

Remove shrimp tails if desired. Place shrimp in a bowl; sprinkle with half of the taco seasoning. Set aside. In another bowl, combine 1/2 cup oil, onion, vinegar, green pepper, garlic, coriander and sugar; set the dressing aside.

In a skillet, stir-fry tortilla strips in remaining oil; drain on paper towels. Sprinkle with remaining taco seasoning. In the same skillet, saute shrimp for 8-10 minutes or until pink.

In a large bowl, combine the greens, tomato, beans, shrimp and tortilla strips. Drizzle with dressing. Sprinkle with cheese; toss. **Yield: 6-8 servings.**

Layered Deli Loaf

German Hot Noodle Salad

Gordon Kremer ✳ SACRAMENTO, CALIFORNIA

Here's a wonderful take on German potato salad. It's flavored like the traditional side dish but uses noodles in place of potatoes. Once my mother served this version, I was hooked.

2	cups wide egg noodles
3	bacon strips
1/4	cup chopped onion
1	tablespoon sugar
1	tablespoon all-purpose flour
1/4	teaspoon salt
1/8	teaspoon ground mustard
1/2	cup water
1/4	cup cider vinegar
1	cup sliced celery
2	tablespoons chopped fresh parsley

Cook noodles according to package directions. Meanwhile, in a large skillet, cook the bacon over medium heat until crisp. Remove the bacon to paper towels to drain, reserving 1 tablespoon drippings. Crumble bacon and set aside.

In the same skillet; saute onion in reserved drippings until tender. Stir in sugar, flour, salt and mustard; add water and vinegar. Cook and stir for 2-3 minutes or until thickened and bubbly.

Rinse and drain noodles; add to skillet. Stir in celery and parsley; heat through. Transfer to a serving bowl; sprinkle with bacon. **Yield: 4 servings.**

German Hot Noodle Salad

Fajita Pitas

Fajita Pitas

Diana Jones ✳ SPRINGTOWN, TEXAS

When I forgot to pick up tortillas for the fajitas we planned for dinner, we used pita bread that I had in the freezer instead. The warm, chicken-filled pockets, garnished with a homemade sauce and other tasty toppings, are often requested when we're hungry for something in a hurry.

6	boneless skinless chicken breast halves (4 ounces *each*)
1	large onion, sliced
1	large green pepper, thinly sliced
1	tablespoon vegetable oil
2	cups (8 ounces) shredded Mexican cheese blend *or* cheddar cheese
8	pita breads (6 inches), halved

SAUCE:

1	medium onion, finely chopped
1	medium tomato, finely chopped
1/2	jalapeno pepper, finely chopped
1	tablespoon minced fresh cilantro
1	tablespoon vegetable oil

Guacamole and sour cream, optional

Grill chicken, covered, over medium heat for 16-20 minutes or until juices run clear, turning occasionally. Cut into strips. In a skillet, saute onion and green pepper in oil. Add chicken and cheese. Stuff into pita halves; place on an ungreased baking sheet. Bake at 325° for 10 minutes or until cheese is melted.

Meanwhile, for sauce, combine the onion, tomato, jalapeno, cilantro and oil in a bowl; mix well. Serve the sauce, guacamole and sour cream if desired with pitas. **Yield: 8 servings.**

EDITOR'S NOTE: When cutting or seeding hot peppers, use rubber or plastic gloves to protect your hands. Avoid touching your face.

2 hot sandwiches

Grilled and juicy...toasted golden in a pan...broiled to melty perfection...whichever way you prepare them, hot sandwiches hit the spot. From tried-and-true classics such as "Ultimate Chicken Sandwiches" to new taste sensations like "Reuben Monte Cristos," this hearty array will fit the bill.

page 23

page 24

page 21

Ultimate Chicken Sandwiches

Ultimate Chicken Sandwiches

Gregg Voss ✳ EMERSON, NEBRASKA

After making these sandwiches, you will never order the fast-food kind again. Marinating the chicken overnight in buttermilk gives it a wonderful taste and tenderness. The zippy breading is golden and crispy.

6	boneless skinless chicken breast halves (4 ounces *each*)
1	cup 1% buttermilk
1/2	cup reduced-fat biscuit/baking mix
1/2	cup cornmeal
1-1/2	teaspoons paprika
3/4	teaspoon salt
3/4	teaspoon poultry seasoning
1/2	teaspoon garlic powder
1/2	teaspoon pepper
1/4	teaspoon cayenne pepper
6	onion *or* kaiser rolls, split
6	lettuce leaves
12	tomato slices

Pound chicken to 1/2-in. thickness. Pour the buttermilk into a large resealable plastic bag; add chicken. Seal bag and turn to coat; refrigerate chicken for 8 hours or overnight.

In a shallow bowl, combine the biscuit mix, cornmeal, paprika, salt, poultry seasoning, garlic powder, pepper and cayenne. Remove chicken one piece at a time, allowing excess buttermilk to drain off. Discard buttermilk. Coat chicken with cornmeal mixture; place in a 13-in. x 9-in. x 2-in. baking dish coated with nonstick cooking spray.

Bake, uncovered, at 400° for 12 minutes. Turn chicken. Bake 8-12 minutes longer or until juices run clear and coating is lightly browned. Serve on rolls with lettuce and tomato. **Yield: 6 servings.**

Reunion Steak Sandwiches

Jan Clark ✳ RIDGEWOOD, NEW JERSEY

Every year, my grandma hosts a family reunion where these flank steak subs steal the show. They're topped with a special sauce that requires only three ingredients. For a quick dinner, serve them with coleslaw and macaroni salad from the deli.

1	beef flank steak (1-1/2 pounds)
1/4	teaspoon salt
1/4	teaspoon pepper
2	tablespoons butter, softened
6	sesame submarine sandwich buns, split
2	medium tomatoes, thinly sliced
1	medium onion, thinly sliced
6	slices process American cheese

MUSTARD SAUCE:

1/2	cup mayonnaise
2	tablespoons Dijon mustard
4-1/2	teaspoons Worcestershire sauce

Sprinkle steak with salt and pepper. Grill, covered, over medium-hot heat for 6-10 minutes on each side or until meat reaches desired doneness (for medium-rare, a meat thermometer should read 145°; medium, 160°; well-done, 170°). Let stand for 5 minutes before thinly slicing.

Spread butter over inside of buns. Place the tomatoes, onion, sliced steak and cheese on bun bottoms. Broil 5-6 in. from the heat for 2-3 minutes or until cheese is melted. In a small bowl, whisk the mayonnaise, mustard and Worcestershire sauce until blended; spoon over cheese. Replace bun tops. **Yield: 6 servings.**

Reunion Steak Sandwiches

Sausage Pepper Sandwiches

Turkey Divan Croissants

Ann Pirrung ✳ CLEVELAND, WISCONSIN

I like to serve these delicious croissants at ladies' luncheons. One time I had leftovers and discovered my fussy family enjoyed them, too.

1/3	cup mayonnaise
1/4	cup Dijon mustard
1-1/2	teaspoons lemon juice
1/2	teaspoon dill weed
1	pound bunch broccoli, finely chopped
1/2	cup chopped onion
2	tablespoons butter
1	cup sliced fresh mushrooms
6	croissants, split
6	ounces thinly sliced cooked turkey
6	slices Swiss cheese

In a small bowl, combine mayonnaise, mustard, lemon juice and dill; set aside.

In a large skillet, saute broccoli and onion in butter for 10 minutes or until tender. Add mushrooms; cook and stir until tender.

Spread mustard mixture over bottom halves of croissants. Top with turkey, broccoli mixture and cheese; replace tops.

Place on a baking sheet. Bake at 350° for 5 minutes or until heated through and cheese is melted. **Yield: 6 servings.**

Sausage Pepper Sandwiches

Suzette Gessel ✳ ALBUQUERQUE, NEW MEXICO

Peppers and onions add fresh flavor to this zesty sausage filling for sandwiches. My mother gave me this recipe. It's simple to assemble, and always gobbled up quickly.

5	uncooked Italian sausage links (about 20 ounces)
1	medium green pepper, cut into 1-inch pieces
1	large onion, cut into 1-inch pieces
1	can (8 ounces) tomato sauce
1/8	teaspoon pepper
6	hoagie *or* submarine sandwich buns, split

In a large skillet, brown sausage links over medium heat. Cut into 1/2-in. slices; place in a 3-qt. slow cooker. Stir in the green pepper, onion, tomato sauce and pepper. Cover and cook on low for 8 hours or until sausage is no longer pink and vegetables are tender. Use a slotted spoon to serve on buns. **Yield: 6 servings.**

Turkey Divan Croissants

tasty TOPPERS

You can easily enhance any sandwich with mouth-watering toppings such as guacamole, salsa, cheese spreads, flavored mayonnaise, Swiss cheese, blue cheese, sauteed mushrooms, tomato slices or strips of crispy bacon.

Luau Chicken Sandwiches

Denise Pope ✳ MISHAWAKA, INDIANA

A friend at work gave me the recipe for this marinade. After grilling the tender chicken a few times for company, I decided to turn it into a sandwich. A pineapple ring and a mild dill and mustard sauce complement it.

USES LESS FAT, SUGAR OR SALT. INCLUDES NUTRITION FACTS.

1	can (20 ounces) sliced pineapple
1	tablespoon brown sugar
1	teaspoon ground mustard
1	teaspoon garlic salt
1/2	teaspoon pepper
6	boneless skinless chicken breast halves (4 ounces *each*)
1/4	cup mayonnaise
1	tablespoon Dijon mustard
1/4	teaspoon dill weed
6	kaiser rolls, split and toasted
6	lettuce leaves, optional

Drain pineapple, reserving 1 cup juice and six pineapple slices (save remaining juice and pineapple for another use). In a large resealable plastic bag, combine the brown sugar, ground mustard, garlic salt, pepper and reserved pineapple juice; add chicken. Seal bag and turn to coat; refrigerate for at least 2 hours, turning occasionally.

In a small bowl, combine the mayonnaise, Dijon mustard and dill. Refrigerate until serving.

Drain and discard marinade. Grill the chicken, covered, over medium heat for 5-6 minutes on each side or until juices run clear. Grill pineapple slices for 1 minute on each side. Spread mayonnaise mixture on rolls. Top with lettuce if desired, chicken and pineapple. **Yield: 6 servings.**

NUTRITION FACTS: 1 sandwich equals 311 calories, 10 g fat (1 g saturated fat), 14 mg cholesterol, 516 mg sodium, 44 g carbohydrate, 2 g fiber, 10 g protein.

Grilled Roast Beef Sandwiches

Grilled Roast Beef Sandwiches

Jolie Goddard ✳ ELKO, NEVADA

This fast favorite hits the spot when we're short on time. Roast beef, cheese and a mixture of sauteed onion, green pepper and mushrooms are tucked between slices of sourdough bread, then toasted to buttery perfection.

1	medium onion, sliced
1	medium green pepper, sliced
1/2	pound fresh mushrooms, sliced
2	to 3 garlic cloves, minced
2	tablespoons vegetable oil
1/4	teaspoon salt
1/8	teaspoon pepper
8	slices sourdough bread
16	slices Colby-Monterey Jack *or* Swiss cheese, *divided*
8	slices deli roast beef
1/2	cup butter, softened

Garlic salt, optional

In a large skillet, saute the onion, green pepper, mushrooms and garlic in oil until tender; sprinkle with salt and pepper. On four slices of bread, layer two slices of cheese, two slices of beef and a fourth of the vegetable mixture. Top with the remaining cheese and bread.

Butter outside of bread; sprinkle with garlic salt if desired. On a hot griddle or large skillet, toast sandwiches for 3-4 minutes on each side or until golden brown. **Yield: 4 servings.**

Luau Chicken Sandwiches

Reuben Monte Cristos

Michelle Rhode ✳ CLEVELAND, OHIO

To put a twist on the traditional Reuben, I dip the sandwiches in egg and crushed corn chips before toasting them. They're great with a cup of soup.

2	eggs
1	tablespoon milk
2-1/2	cups corn chips, crushed
8	slices rye bread
1/2	cup Thousand Island salad dressing
12	slices deli corned beef
8	slices Swiss cheese
1	cup sauerkraut, rinsed and well drained

In a shallow bowl, beat the eggs and milk. Place chips in another shallow bowl. Dip one side of four slices of bread in the egg mixture, then in the chips. Place chip side down on a greased baking sheet. Spread salad dressing on each slice. Layer each with one slice corned beef, one slice Swiss cheese and 1/4 cup sauerkraut.

Dip one side of the remaining bread slices in the egg mixture and chips; place bread chip side up on sandwiches.

On a large skillet or griddle, toast sandwiches over medium-high heat for 4-5 minutes on each side or until bread is lightly browned and cheese is melted. **Yield: 4 servings.**

Ham and Swiss Stromboli

Pat Raport ✳ GAINESVILLE, FLORIDA

This pretty, swirled loaf is simple and versatile. Fill it with anything your family likes. Try sliced pepperoni and provolone cheese, or anchovies and ripe olives if you're feeling adventurous.

1	tube (11 ounces) refrigerated crusty French loaf
6	ounces thinly sliced deli ham
6	green onions, sliced
8	bacon strips, cooked and crumbled
1-1/2	cups (6 ounces) shredded Swiss cheese

Unroll dough on a greased baking sheet. Place ham over dough to within 1/2 in. of edges; sprinkle evenly with onions, bacon and cheese. Roll up jelly-roll style, starting with a long side. Pinch seams to seal and tuck ends under. Place seam side down on baking sheet.

Ham and Swiss Stromboli

With a sharp knife, cut several 1/4-in.-deep slits on top of loaf. Bake at 350° for 26-30 minutes or until golden brown. Cool slightly before slicing. Serve warm. **Yield: 8 servings.**

Hot Colby Ham Sandwiches

Sherry Crenshaw ✳ FORT WORTH, TEXAS

This yummy recipe is a winner with friends and family. Not only are the warm sandwiches a snap to prepare, but they smell so good when baking that no one can resist them. They're a staple at our get-togethers.

1/2	cup butter, melted
2	tablespoons prepared mustard
1	tablespoon dried minced onion
1	tablespoon poppy seeds
2	to 3 teaspoons sugar
8	hamburger buns, split
8	slices Colby cheese
16	slices thinly sliced deli ham (about 1 pound)
1-1/2	cups (6 ounces) shredded part-skim mozzarella cheese

In a small bowl, combine butter, mustard, onion, poppy seeds and sugar. Place roll bottoms, cut side up, in an ungreased 15-in. x 10-in. x 1-in. baking pan. Top each with one slice of Colby cheese, two slices of ham and mozzarella. Brush with half of the butter mixture. Replace roll tops. Brush the tops of the rolls with remaining butter mixture. Bake, uncovered, at 350° for 10-15 minutes or until cheese is melted. **Yield: 15 servings.**

Asparagus Chicken Sandwiches

Asparagus Chicken Sandwiches

Anca Cretan ✳ HAGERSTOWN, MARYLAND

No one will be able to resist these lovely open-faced delights that definitely say "spring." Served on toasted English muffins, slices of chicken and tomato are topped with fresh asparagus spears, then draped with a creamy lemon sauce. This is a great way to use leftover chicken or turkey.

USES LESS FAT, SUGAR OR SALT. INCLUDES NUTRITION FACTS.

1	pound fresh asparagus, trimmed and cut into 3-inch pieces
1-1/2	cups reduced-fat sour cream
2	teaspoons lemon juice
1-1/2	teaspoons prepared mustard
1/2	teaspoon salt
8	ounces sliced cooked chicken breast
4	English muffins, split and toasted
2	medium tomatoes, sliced

Paprika, optional

Place asparagus in a saucepan and cover with water; bring to a boil. Cover and cook for 2 minutes or until crisp-tender. Drain and set aside. In the same pan, combine the sour cream, lemon juice, mustard and salt; cook on low until heated through. Remove from the heat.

Place chicken on a microwave-safe plate; microwave on high for 30-40 seconds or until warmed. Place two English muffin halves on each serving plate. Top with chicken, tomatoes, asparagus and sauce. Sprinkle with paprika if desired. **Yield: 4 servings.**

NUTRITION FACTS: 2 topped muffin halves equals 385 calories, 11 g fat (7 g saturated fat), 78 mg cholesterol, 645 mg sodium, 40 g carbohydrate, 2 g fiber, 32 g protein.

EDITOR'S NOTE: This recipe was tested in a 1,100-watt microwave.

Grill Bread

Taste of Home Test Kitchen ✳ GREENDALE, WISCONSIN

When you want fresh flavors, but something a little different, try this. Sliced veggies top tender bread that's "baked" to perfection on the grill.

4	frozen Texas rolls (2 ounces *each*), thawed
2	garlic cloves, minced
2	tablespoons olive oil
1/2	pound fresh mushrooms, sliced
1	small onion, cut into thin wedges
1	medium green pepper, sliced
1	medium sweet yellow pepper, sliced
1	medium sweet red pepper, sliced
1/2	cup fresh snow peas
3/4	teaspoon salt
1/8	teaspoon pepper
1/2	teaspoon dried oregano

On a lightly floured surface, roll out each roll into an 8-in. to 10-in. circle, turning dough frequently; set aside.

In a large skillet, saute garlic in oil until tender. Add mushrooms; saute for 2-3 minutes. Add onion, peppers, peas, salt, pepper and oregano; stir-fry until vegetables are crisp-tender, about 3 minutes.

Meanwhile, grill bread, uncovered, over medium-high heat for 30-45 seconds on each side or until lightly browned. Fill with vegetable mixture and serve immediately. The bread can be reheated in the microwave. **Yield: 4 servings.**

Grill Bread

Fried Green Tomato Sandwiches

2-1/2 cups shredded cooked chicken
1/4 cup lemon juice
1/4 cup soy sauce
2 tablespoons sugar
1 tablespoon brown sugar
3/4 teaspoon minced garlic
1/2 teaspoon ground ginger
4 sandwich buns, split

In a large saucepan, combine the first seven ingredients. Bring to a boil. Reduce heat; simmer, uncovered, for 3-4 minutes or until heated through. Spoon chicken mixture onto each bun bottom; replace tops. **Yield: 4 servings.**

Fried Green Tomato Sandwiches

Mary Ann Bostic ✳ SINKS GROVE, WEST VIRGINIA

This is one of my favorite quick-to-fix suppers. If you've never tried fried green tomatoes, give them a shot with these sandwiches. They're yummy!

1/4 cup all-purpose flour
1/4 teaspoon *each* garlic powder, salt, pepper and paprika
3 medium green tomatoes, sliced
12 bacon strips
12 slices sourdough bread, toasted
6 slices provolone cheese
Leaf lettuce, mayonnaise and Dijon mustard

In a shallow dish, combine flour and seasonings; dip tomatoes in the mixture and set aside. In a large skillet, cook bacon over medium heat until crisp.

Remove to paper towels to drain. In the drippings, cook tomatoes for 2 minutes on each side; drain on paper towels.

Place six slices of toast on a baking sheet. Layer with three tomato slices, two bacon strips and a provolone cheese slice. Broil 3-4 in. from the heat for 3-4 minutes or until the cheese is melted. Top with lettuce if desired.

Spread mayonnaise and mustard on remaining toast if desired; place over lettuce. **Yield: 6 sandwiches.**

Teriyaki Chicken Sandwiches

Pam May ✳ AUBURN, ALABAMA

Lemon juice, soy sauce, garlic, ginger and a touch of brown sugar create a lip-smacking sauce that seasons shredded cooked chicken.

Hot Pizza Subs

Anna Whelan ✳ CRYSTAL, NORTH DAKOTA

I stack this warm sub with a mountain of ingredients...you'll have to open wide to take a bite! Slices are hearty with ham, melted cheese, salami and pepperoni.

1 unsliced loaf (1 pound) Italian bread
1/4 cup pizza sauce
1-1/2 teaspoons Italian seasoning
1 medium green pepper, thinly sliced
4 slices fully cooked ham
10 slices salami
30 slices pepperoni
4 slices *each* cheddar, part-skim mozzarella and American cheese

Slice bread in half horizontally. Spread bottom half with pizza sauce; sprinkle with Italian seasoning. Top with green pepper, ham, salami, pepperoni and cheese; replace bread top. Place on a baking sheet. Bake at 425° for 12-15 minutes or until cheese is melted. **Yield: 4 servings.**

Hot Pizza Subs

Taco Sandwich

Melody Stoltzfus ✳ PARKESBURG, PENNSYLVANIA

This is like a taco on French bread. It's great when you don't have taco shells or tortillas on hand. The salsa-cream cheese spread adds a delicious kick.

- 1 pound ground beef
- 1 loaf (1 pound) unsliced Italian bread
- 4 ounces cream cheese, softened
- 1/2 cup salsa
- 2 tablespoons taco seasoning
- 1 cup shredded lettuce
- 1 large tomato, sliced
- 6 slices American cheese

In a large skillet, cook beef over medium heat until no longer pink. Meanwhile, cut bread in half lengthwise; hollow out top and bottom of loaf, leaving a 1/2-in. shell (discard removed bread or save for another use). In a small mixing bowl, beat cream cheese and salsa until blended. Spread inside bread shell; set aside.

Drain beef. Stir in taco seasoning. Layer the lettuce and tomato in bottom of bread shell; top with beef mixture and American cheese. Replace bread top. **Yield: 6 servings.**

Taco Sandwich

- 4 slices tomato
- 4 slices onion
- 4 teaspoons sweet *or* dill pickle relish
- 4 hamburger buns, split

In a large bowl, beat the eggs, salt and pepper; crumble beef over mixture and mix well. Shape into eight thin patties.

Layer four patties with the tomato, onion and relish. Top with remaining patties and press edges firmly to seal. Broil 4-6 in. from the heat for 8 minutes on each side or until no meat is longer pink. Serve over buns. **Yield: 4 servings.**

EDITOR'S NOTE: Before broiling foods, spray broiler pan with nonstick cooking spray or line it with greased foil. Cleanup will be quick with little mess.

Stuffed Half-Pounders

June Croft ✳ BAY MINETTE, ALABAMA

We made these big bites in my high school home economics class back in the 1960s. Traditional toppings are cleverly tucked inside these plump burgers for a mouthful of wonderful flavor.

- 2 eggs, lightly beaten

Salt and pepper to taste

- 2 pounds ground beef

Stuffed Half-Pounders

Tropical Tuna Melts

Renee Sagmoe ✳ CHAMPLIN, MINNESOTA

Bring the taste of the Caribbean to your kitchen with these open-faced rave-winners. Pineapple rings add a tangy twist to traditional tuna melts. Consider replacing the English muffins with bagels.

- 1 to 2 tablespoons mayonnaise
- 1 to 2 tablespoons finely chopped celery
- 1/4 to 1/2 teaspoon salt
- 1/8 to 1/4 teaspoon lemon-pepper seasoning
- 1 can (6 ounces) tuna, drained and flaked
- 2 English muffins, split and toasted
- 1 can (8 ounces) sliced pineapple, drained
- 4 slices process American cheese

In a large bowl, combine the mayonnaise, celery, salt and lemon-pepper; stir in tuna. Spread over muffin halves. Top each with a slice of pineapple and cheese. Broil 4-6 in. from the heat for 2 minutes or until cheese is melted and lightly browned. **Yield: 2-4 servings.**

Italian Pork Hoagies

Jackie Hannahs ✳ FOUNTAIN, MICHIGAN

I like to prepare these quick, toasted hoagies whenever I have extra pork. I spread pizza sauce over the buns before adding sliced pork, Italian salad dressing and mozzarella cheese.

6	hoagie buns, split
1/2	cup pizza sauce
12	slices cooked pork (1/4 inch thick and 2 ounces *each*)
1/2	cup Italian salad dressing
1/2	cup shredded part-skim mozzarella cheese

Place botom and top halves of buns cut side up on a baking sheet. Spread pizza sauce on the bottom half of each bun. Top with pork; drizzle with salad dressing. Sprinkle with cheese.

Bake at 350° for 5-10 minutes or until cheese is melted and tops of buns are lightly toasted. Replace bun tops. **Yield: 6 servings.**

Italian Pork Hoagies

Raspberry Chicken Sandwiches

Kelly Williams ✳ LA PORTE, INDIANA

The sweet-and-sassy raspberry barbecue sauce makes these grilled chicken specialties simply outstanding. I also use this sauce on meatballs, chicken wings and pork chops.

1	cup chili sauce
3/4	cup raspberry preserves
2	tablespoons red wine vinegar
1	tablespoon Dijon mustard
6	boneless skinless chicken breast halves (4 ounces *each*)
2	tablespoons plus 1/2 cup olive oil, *divided*
1/2	teaspoon salt
1/4	teaspoon pepper
24	slices French bread (1/2 inch thick)
12	slices Muenster cheese, halved

Shredded lettuce

Coat grill rack with nonstick cooking spray before starting the grill. In a small saucepan, combine the first four ingredients. Bring to a boil. Reduce heat; simmer, uncovered, for 2 minutes. Set aside 1 cup for serving and remaining sauce for basting.

Flatten chicken breasts to 1/4-in. thickness. Cut in half widthwise; place in a large resealable plastic bag. Add 2 tablespoons oil, salt and pepper. Seal bag and turn to coat. Brush remaining oil over both sides of bread.

Grill chicken, uncovered, over medium heat for 5-7 minutes on each side or until the juices run clear, basting frequently with raspberry sauce. Remove and keep warm.

Grill bread, uncovered, for 1-2 minutes or until lightly browned on one side. Turn and top each piece of bread with a slice of cheese. Grill 1-2 minutes longer or until bottom of bread is toasted. Place a piece of chicken, lettuce and reserved raspberry sauce on half of bread slices; top with remaining bread. **Yield: 12 servings.**

Raspberry Chicken Sandwiches

Honey-Citrus Chicken Sandwiches

Honey-Citrus Chicken Sandwiches

Claire Batherson ✳ WESTCHESTER, ILLINOIS

During the summer months, our kids keep me busy. So it's a welcome relief when my husband volunteers to cook out. This is his specialty.

6	boneless skinless chicken breast halves (4 ounces *each*)
1/4	cup orange juice
1/4	cup lemon juice
1/4	cup honey
2	tablespoons vegetable oil
1	tablespoon prepared mustard
1/4	teaspoon poultry seasoning
1/8	to 1/4 teaspoon cayenne pepper
6	slices Monterey Jack *or* Muenster cheese, optional
6	kaiser rolls, split
6	thin tomato slices
6	red onion slices

Shredded lettuce

Flatten chicken breast evenly to 1/4-in. thickness; set aside. In a large resealable plastic bag, combine the orange and lemon juices, honey, oil, mustard, poultry seasoning and cayenne pepper. Add chicken breasts; seal bag and turn to coat. Refrigerate chicken for 6-8 hours or overnight.

Drain; discard marinade. Grill, uncovered, over medium-low heat, turning occasionally, for 10-12 minutes or until juices run clear. If desired, top each chicken breast with a slice of cheese and grill 1-2 minutes longer or until cheese begins to melt. Serve on rolls with tomato, onion and lettuce. **Yield: 6 servings.**

Curry Cheddar Grill

Mary Engelmeyer ✳ WEST POINT, NEBRASKA

As a farm wife with three active teenagers, I need recipes that call for common ingredients and that can be put together quickly. I've come to rely on this snappy grilled cheese.

1/2	cup mayonnaise
1/4	cup mango chutney
1	to 1-1/2 teaspoons curry powder
3/4	teaspoon salt
2	cups finely shredded cabbage
12	slices rye bread
12	slices (1 ounce *each*) fully cooked ham
1/2	pound cheddar cheese, cut into 6 thin slices
1/4	cup butter, softened

In a large bowl, combine the mayonnaise, chutney, curry powder and salt; stir in cabbage. On six slices of bread, layer two slices of ham, one slice of cheese and 1/4 cup cabbage mixture; top with remaining bread. Butter outsides of each sandwich.

In a large skillet or griddle, melt 2-3 tablespoons butter. Toast sandwiches in batches until bread is lightly browned on both sides, adding remaining butter when necessary. **Yield: 6 servings.**

Dilly Chicken Sandwiches

Orien Major ✳ HINTON, ALBERTA

A creamy lemon-dill spread adds summery flavor to tender chicken served between slices of grilled French bread.

4	boneless skinless chicken breast halves (4 ounces *each*)
1	garlic clove, minced
3/4	teaspoon dill weed, *divided*
6	tablespoons butter, *divided*
8	slices French bread (1/2 inch thick)
1/4	cup cream cheese, softened
2	teaspoons lemon juice
4	lettuce leaves
8	slices tomato

Flatten chicken to 1/4-in. thickness; set aside. In a large skillet, saute garlic and 1/2 teaspoon dill in 3 tablespoons butter. Add chicken; cook over medium heat until chicken juices run clear. Remove and keep warm.

Spread both sides of bread with remaining but-

Dilly Chicken Sandwiches

ter. In a skillet or griddle, grill bread on both sides until golden brown. Meanwhile in a small bowl, combine the cream cheese, lemon juice and remaining dill; spread on one side of grilled bread. Place lettuce, chicken and tomato on four slices of bread; top with remaining bread. **Yield: 4 servings.**

Grilled Sub Sandwich

Char Shanahan ✳ SCHERERVILLE, INDIANA

After a long, hard day at band camp, my daughter comes home with a huge appetite. This grilled sub satisfies my hungry marcher! It's also easy to prepare.

1	large green pepper, thinly sliced
1	small onion, thinly sliced and separated into rings
1/2	teaspoon olive oil
1	loaf (1 pound) unsliced Italian bread
1/3	cup prepared Italian salad dressing, *divided*
2	ounces sliced deli turkey
4	slices Swiss cheese
2	ounces sliced deli ham
3	slices cheddar cheese
2	ounces sliced deli pastrami
1/2	cup sliced dill pickles
1	large tomato, thinly sliced

Additional olive oil

In a large bowl, toss green pepper and onion with oil. Place on a double thickness of heavy-duty foil (about 12-in. square). Fold foil around vegetables and seal tightly. Grill, covered, over medium-hot heat for 12-15 minutes or until tender; set aside.

Cut loaf in half horizontally; remove bread from top half, leaving a 1/2-in. shell (discard removed bread or save for another use). Brush cut sides of loaf with salad dressing; place cut side down on grill. Grill, uncovered, over medium heat for 3-5 minutes or until golden brown.

Place bottom of loaf on a double thickness of heavy-duty foil (about 18 in. x 12 in.). Layer with turkey, two slices of Swiss cheese, ham, cheddar cheese, pastrami and remaining Swiss cheese. Top with green pepper mixture, pickles and tomato.

Drizzle remaining dressing over cut side of bread top; place over filling. Brush bread with additional oil. Fold foil around sandwich and seal tightly. Grill, covered, over medium heat for 4-8 minutes or until cheese is melted. Cut into slices with a serrated knife. **Yield: 4 servings.**

Grilled Sub Sandwich

grilling GADGETS

If you enjoy grilled sandwiches, you may want to invest in an electric or stovetop griddle. Not only can you grill four to six sandwiches at a time, but you can also fry up bacon, sliced onions and other warm sandwich toppings.

Lasagna Sandwiches

Gail Rotheiser ✳ HIGHLAND PARK, ILLINOIS

These cheesy, toasted favorites really taste like lasagna. They're perfect for a fast evening meal—our children loved them with vegetable soup and crunchy potato sticks.

1/4	cup sour cream
2	tablespoons chopped onion
1/2	teaspoon dried oregano
1/4	teaspoon seasoned salt
8	slices Italian *or* other white bread
8	bacon strips, halved and cooked
8	slices tomato
4	slices part-skim mozzarella cheese
2	to 3 tablespoons butter

In a small bowl, combine the first four ingredients; spread on four slices of bread. Layer each with four strips of bacon, two tomato slices and a slice of cheese; top with remaining bread.

   In a large skillet or griddle, melt 2-3 tablespoons butter. Toast sandwiches until bread is lightly browned on both sides, adding butter if necessary. **Yield: 4 servings.**

Lasagna Sandwiches

Pizza Loaf

Jenny Brown ✳ WEST LAFAYETTE, INDIANA

This savory stromboli relies on frozen bread dough, so it comes together in no time. The golden loaf is stuffed with cheese, pepperoni, mushrooms, peppers and olives. I often add a few slices of ham, too. It's tasty served with warm pizza sauce for dipping.

Pizza Loaf

1	loaf (1 pound) frozen bread dough, thawed
2	eggs, *separated*
1	tablespoon grated Parmesan cheese
1	tablespoon olive oil
1	teaspoon minced fresh parsley
1	teaspoon dried oregano
1/2	teaspoon garlic powder
1/4	teaspoon pepper
8	ounces sliced pepperoni
2	cups (8 ounces) shredded part-skim mozzarella cheese
1	can (4 ounces) mushroom stems and pieces, drained
1/4	to 1/2 cup pickled pepper rings
1	medium green pepper, diced
1	can (2-1/4 ounces) sliced ripe olives
1	can (15 ounces) pizza sauce

On a greased baking sheet, roll out dough into a 15-in. x 10-in. rectangle. In a small bowl, combine the egg yolks, Parmesan cheese, oil, parsley, oregano, garlic powder and pepper. Brush over the bread dough.

   Sprinkle dough with pepperoni, mozzarella cheese, mushrooms, pepper rings, green pepper and olives. Roll up, jelly-roll style, starting with a long side; pinch seam to seal and tuck ends under.

   Place seam side down; brush with egg whites. Do not let rise. Bake at 350° for 35-40 minutes or until golden brown. Warm the pizza sauce; serve with sliced loaf. **Yield: 10-12 slices.**

Baked Deli Sandwich

Sandra McKenzie ✳ BRAHAM, MINNESOTA

Frozen bread dough, easy assembly and a quick baking time make this stuffed loaf a recipe I rely on often. It's easy to double for a crowd or to experiment with different meats and cheeses.

1	loaf (1 pound) frozen bread dough, thawed
2	tablespoons butter, melted
1/4	teaspoon garlic salt
1/4	teaspoon dried basil
1/4	teaspoon dried oregano
1/4	teaspoon pizza seasoning *or* Italian seasoning
1/4	pound sliced deli ham
6	thin slices part-skim mozzarella cheese
1/4	pound sliced deli smoked turkey breast
6	thin slices cheddar cheese

Pizza sauce, warmed, optional

On a baking sheet coated with nonstick cooking spray, roll dough into a small rectangle. Let rest for 5-10 minutes.

In a small bowl, combine the butter and seasonings. Roll out dough into a 14-in. x 10-in. rectangle. Brush with half of the butter mixture. Layer the

Baked Deli Sandwich

ham, mozzarella cheese, turkey and cheddar cheese lengthwise over half of the dough to within 1/2 in. of edges. Fold dough over and pinch firmly to seal. Brush with remaining butter mixture.

Bake at 400° for 10-12 minutes or until golden brown. Cut into 1-in. slices. Serve immediately with pizza sauce if desired. **Yield: 4-6 servings.**

Pumpkin Burgers

Linda Shuttleworth ✳ CIRCLEVILLE, OHIO

In our town, we have a pumpkin festival in late October and use pumpkins in many different ways. This is a popular recipe for "sandwich night" at our house.

1-1/2	pounds ground beef
1	medium onion, chopped
1	bottle (12 ounces) chili sauce
1	can (10-3/4 ounces) condensed tomato soup, undiluted
1/2	cup canned pumpkin
1	teaspoon salt
1/2	to 1 teaspoon pumpkin pie spice
1/4	teaspoon pepper
6	to 8 hamburger buns, split

In a large skillet, cook beef and onion over medium heat until meat is no longer pink; drain. Add the chili sauce, soup, pumpkin, salt, pumpkin pie spice and pepper. Bring to a boil. Reduce heat; cover and simmer for 1 hour or until thickened. Serve on buns. **Yield: 6-8 servings.**

Pumpkin Burgers

3 cold sandwiches

For a quick lunch, light supper or late-night snack, these cold sandwich creations are the perfect fare. Sink your teeth into deli meats and cheeses piled high on submarine rolls...open wide for a tasty club...savor fresh salads on a croissant...any way you slice them, these bites are delicious!

page 42

page 41

page 35

Turkey Salad Croissants

Turkey Salad Croissants

Kim Due ✳ FRIEND, NEBRASKA

I keep this creamy-crunchy mixture on hand for lunches and after-school snacks. It's a great way to use up leftover turkey and make the most of homegrown vegetables.

2	cups cubed cooked turkey
1/2	cup chopped celery
1/2	cup chopped cashews
1/2	cup mayonnaise
1/4	cup coarsely chopped radishes
2	tablespoons chopped green onions
2	tablespoons diced pimientos
1	tablespoon lemon juice
1	teaspoon dill weed
1	teaspoon seasoned salt

Lettuce leaves
| 6 | croissants, split |

In a large bowl, combine the first 10 ingredients. Place lettuce and 2/3 cup turkey salad on each croissant. **Yield: 6 servings.**

Lunch Box Special

Bernice Morris ✳ MARSHFIELD, MISSOURI

Dates, orange juice and apples bring zest and texture to the plain old peanut butter sandwich. The wonderful sweet-salty combination is a treat.

1/2	cup peanut butter
1/4	cup orange juice
1/2	cup finely chopped apples
1/2	cup finely chopped dates
1/2	cup chopped walnuts, optional
8	slices bread

In a bowl, combine the peanut butter and orange juice until blended. Add the apples, dates and walnuts if desired. Spread on four slices of bread; top with remaining bread. **Yield: 4 servings.**

Avocado Ham Sandwiches

Toby Raymond ✳ SPRINGFIELD, OREGON

An avocado spread adds mild flavor and delicate color to this ham and cheese sandwich. You can toast or grill the bread. It's a hit with our family.

1	medium ripe avocado, peeled and mashed
2	tablespoons mayonnaise

Dash cayenne pepper
12	slices whole wheat *or* sourdough bread
6	slices fully cooked ham
6	slices Swiss cheese
6	tablespoons cream cheese, softened

In a small bowl, combine the first three ingredients; spread on six slices of bread. Top with ham and Swiss. Spread cream cheese on remaining bread; place over Swiss cheese. **Yield: 6 servings.**

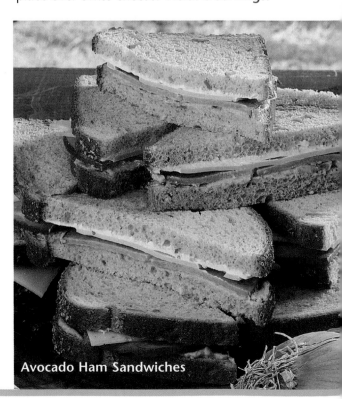
Avocado Ham Sandwiches

Greek Hero

1/4   cup thinly sliced red onion
1/4   cup chopped ripe olives
1/4   cup chopped stuffed olives
1/2   cup crumbled feta cheese
4   lettuce leaves

For hummus, in a food processor, combine the lemon juice, oil and beans; cover and process until smooth. Stir in the garlic, oregano, salt and pepper.

Slice bread in half horizontally. Carefully hollow out bottom half, leaving a 1/2-in. shell. Spread hummus into shell. Layer with the red peppers, cucumber, tomatoes, onion, olives, cheese and lettuce. Replace bread top. Cut into four portions. **Yield: 4 servings.**

Greek Hero

Margaret Wilson ✳ HEMET, CALIFORNIA

This Greek-style sandwich is made by spreading a loaf of bread with hummus, veggies, seasonings and feta cheese. With plenty of refreshing fillings and a hearty bean spread that packs in protein, this stacked submarine makes a satisfying meal-in-one.

HUMMUS:

2   tablespoons lemon juice
1   tablespoon olive oil
1   can (15 ounces) garbanzo beans *or* chickpeas, rinsed and drained
2   garlic cloves, minced
1   teaspoon dried oregano
1/4   teaspoon salt
1/8   teaspoon pepper

SANDWICH:

1   loaf (8 ounces) unsliced French bread
2   medium sweet red peppers, cut into thin strips
1/2   medium cucumber, sliced
2   small tomatoes, sliced

Fancy Ham 'n' Cheese

James Gauthier ✳ OAK CREEK, WISCONSIN

Garden-fresh ingredients including spinach, cucumber and onion add appeal to this zippy ham sandwich. It turns the ordinary into something special.

1/4   cup butter, softened
8   slices rye bread
12   fresh spinach leaves
16   cucumber slices
4   thin slices red onion
12   slices fully cooked ham
2   tablespoons Dijon mustard
8   slices cheddar cheese

Spread butter on one side of each slice of bread. On half of the slices, layer spinach, cucumber, onion, ham, mustard and cheese. Top with remaining bread. **Yield: 4 servings.**

flavor SAVOR

Hummus is a Mediterranean spread that offers a tasty change of pace from mayonnaise or mustard. It usually combines garbanzo beans with lemon juice, olive oil and garlic, but feel free to add your favorite herbs or seasonings.

Fancy Ham 'n' Cheese

Barbecued Chicken Salad Sandwiches

Linda Orme ✳ BATTLEGROUND, WASHINGTON

An impromptu picnic inspired me to put together this dressed-up chicken salad sandwich. The barbecue sauce gives the poultry a scrumptious punch. An instant summertime favorite, these sandwiches have become a mainstay at our house.

1-1/2	pounds boneless skinless chicken breast
1/2	cup barbecue sauce
1	cup mayonnaise
1/2	cup finely chopped onion
1/2	cup chopped celery
1/4	teaspoon salt
1/4	teaspoon crushed red pepper flakes
8	kaiser rolls, split
8	lettuce leaves
8	tomato slices

Place the chicken in a large resealable plastic bag; add barbecue sauce. Seal the bag and turn to coat. Refrigerate overnight.

Grill chicken, covered, over medium-hot heat for 6-8 minutes on each side or until juices run clear. Cool; cover and refrigerate chicken until chilled.

Chop chicken; place in a bowl. Stir in the mayonnaise, onion, celery, salt and pepper flakes. Serve on rolls with lettuce and tomato. **Yield: 8 servings.**

Italian Subs

Barbecued Chicken Salad Sandwiches

Italian Subs

Delores Christner ✳ SPOONER, WISCONSIN

Olive-lovers are sure to rejoice over this stacked creation! Stuffed and ripe olives are marinated in white wine vinegar and garlic before using them to flavor these speedy salami, ham and provolone subs. They're perfect for hearty appetites.

1/3	cup olive oil
4-1/2	teaspoons white wine vinegar
1	tablespoon dried parsley flakes
2	to 3 garlic cloves, minced
1	can (2-1/4 ounces) sliced ripe olives, drained
1/2	cup sliced pimiento-stuffed olives
6	submarine sandwich buns (10 inches), split
24	thin slices hard salami
24	sliced provolone cheese
24	thin slices fully cooked ham

Lettuce leaves, optional

In a small bowl, combine the oil, vinegar, parsley and garlic. Stir in olives. Cover and refrigerate for 8 hours or overnight.

Place about 2 tablespoons olive mixture on the bottom of each bun. Top each with four slices of salami, cheese and ham; add lettuce if desired. Replace tops. **Yield: 6 servings.**

Pepper Lover's BLT

Carol Reaves ✳ SAN ANTONIO, TEXAS

One of my family's most-requested sandwiches is a BLT, and they especially love this one because it combines the tantalizing combination of bacon and fresh tomatoes with hot peppers.

1/4	cup mayonnaise
1	tablespoon diced pimientos

1/8	teaspoon coarsely ground pepper
1/4	teaspoon hot pepper sauce
8	slices sourdough bread, toasted
4	teaspoons Dijon-mayonnaise blend
6	tablespoons shredded sharp cheddar cheese
4	pickled jalapeno peppers *or* green chilies, thinly sliced
12	bacon strips, cooked and drained
8	tomato slices
4	lettuce leaves
8	thin slices cooked turkey

In a small bowl, combine the mayonnaise, pimientos, pepper and pepper sauce. Chill for at least 1 hour.

Spread four slices of toast with Dijon-mayonnaise blend. Sprinkle with the cheese; top with jalapenos, bacon, tomato, lettuce and turkey. Spread mayonnaise mixture on remaining toast; place over turkey. **Yield: 4 servings.**

Vegetable Tuna Sandwiches

Mrs. Allan Miller ✳ ST. JOHN, NEW BRUNSWICK

I packed lunches for a husband and seven children for years and tried different recipes such as this to keep things new and exciting.

2	packages (3 ounces each) cream cheese, softened, *divided*
6	tablespoons mayonnaise, *divided*
1/4	teaspoon salt
1/8	teaspoon pepper
1	can (6 ounces) tuna, drained and flaked
3	tablespoons finely chopped celery
3	tablespoons finely chopped green pepper
1	cup shredded carrots
2	tablespoons finely chopped onion
8	slices white bread
4	slices whole wheat bread

In a large bowl, combine one package of cream cheese, 3 tablespoons mayonnaise, salt and pepper until smooth. Stir in the tuna, celery and green pepper. In another bowl, combine the carrots, onion and remaining cream cheese and mayonnaise. Spread 1/3 cup tuna mixture on four slices of white bread; top with a slice of whole wheat bread. Spread 1/4 cup carrot mixture on the whole wheat bread; top with a slice of white bread. **Yield: 4 servings.**

Waldorf Turkey Sandwiches

Meghan Bodas ✳ RAPID CITY, SOUTH DAKOTA

Apples, celery and raisins give this special turkey salad a great flavor and tempting texture. If you enjoy Waldorf salad, you're sure to become a fan of this creation, too.

USES LESS FAT, SUGAR OR SALT. INCLUDES NUTRITION FACTS.

1/4	cup finely chopped celery
3	tablespoons fat-free mayonnaise
2	tablespoons fat-free plain yogurt
2	tablespoons chopped walnuts
1	tablespoon raisins
1/8	teaspoon ground nutmeg
1/8	teaspoon ground cinnamon
1-1/4	cups cubed cooked turkey breast
1	small apple, chopped
8	slices cinnamon-raisin bread, toasted
4	lettuce leaves

In a large bowl, combine the first seven ingredients. Add turkey and apple; toss to coat. Cover and refrigerate for 1 hour. Spoon 3/4 cup turkey mixture onto four slices of bread; top with a lettuce leaf and remaining bread. **Yield: 4 servings.**

NUTRITION FACTS: 3/4 cup turkey salad (calculated without bread) equals 127 calories, 5 g fat (0 saturated fat), 26 mg cholesterol, 114 mg sodium, 9 g carbohydrate, 0 fiber, 12 g protein.

Waldorf Turkey Sandwiches

Special Eggplant Subs

Special Eggplant Subs

Marie Maffucci ✳ NEW ROCHELLE, NEW YORK

The idea for this unique recipe was inspired by a light eggplant dish I made for hot summer evenings. I decided to use the golden eggplant slices as a base for sandwiches.

2	eggs
1	cup dry bread crumbs
1	medium eggplant, peeled and sliced 1/4 inch thick
4	submarine sandwich buns (10 inches), split

Leaf lettuce

1	jar (7-1/4 ounces) roasted red peppers, drained and sliced
8	slices part-skim mozzarella cheese
2	medium tomatoes, thinly sliced
1	can (2-1/4 ounces) chopped ripe olives, drained

Italian *or* vinaigrette salad dressing

In a shallow bowl, beat the eggs. Place bread crumbs in another bowl. Dip eggplant slices into egg, then coat with crumbs. Place on a greased baking sheet.

Bake at 350° for 30 minutes or until crispy. Cool. On the bottom of each bun, layer lettuce, eggplant, red peppers, cheese, tomatoes and olives. Drizzle with salad dressing; replace bun tops. **Yield: 4 servings.**

California Clubs

Diane Cigel ✳ STEVENS POINT, WISCONSIN

Ranch dressing and Dijon mustard create a tangy sauce to top this sandwich. Pairing tomato and avocado with the chicken and bacon is just the right combination on sourdough bread.

1/2	cup ranch salad dressing
1/4	cup Dijon mustard
8	slices sourdough bread, toasted
4	boneless skinless chicken breast halves, cooked and sliced
1	large tomato, sliced
1	medium ripe avocado, peeled and sliced
12	bacon strips, cooked and drained

In a small bowl, combine salad dressing and mustard; spread on each slice of bread. On four slices of bread, layer the chicken, tomato, avocado and bacon. Top with remaining bread. **Yield: 4 servings.**

Chicken-Apple Croissants

Tobi Breternitz ✳ BAY PORT, MICHIGAN

The sweet-tart flavors of juicy apples and grapes really jazz up my version of chicken salad. Serve it on croissants or hard rolls.

2	cups diced cooked chicken
1	cup diced peeled apple
3/4	cup mayonnaise
1/2	cup halved green grapes
1/4	cup sliced almonds, toasted
1/2	teaspoon seasoned salt
1/4	teaspoon pepper
6	croissants *or* hard rolls, split
6	lettuce leaves

In a bowl, combine the first seven ingredients. Spoon about 1/2 cup onto each croissant; top with lettuce. **Yield: 6 servings.**

Turkey Cranwich

Judy Benson ✳ CAPRON, ILLINOIS

When my mother-in-law and I put Thanksgiving leftovers between slices of sourdough bread, we knew we had a new family favorite.

2	tablespoons cream cheese, softened
4	slices sourdough bread
1/4	cup chopped walnuts
1/3	pound thinly sliced cooked turkey
1/4	cup whole-berry cranberry sauce
2	slices Swiss cheese

Lettuce leaves

Spread the cream cheese on two slices of bread. Sprinkle with walnuts. Top with turkey; spread cranberry sauce over turkey. Top with the Swiss cheese, lettuce and remaining bread. **Yield: 2 servings.**

Berry Turkey Sandwich

Berry Turkey Sandwich

Edward Meyer ✳ ARNOLD, MISSOURI

Sliced fresh strawberries, Swiss cheese and a nutty cream cheese spread make this turkey sandwich different. Try it on whole wheat, oatmeal or even sunflower seed bread.

4	slices whole wheat bread
2	lettuce leaves
2	slices reduced-fat Swiss cheese
1/4	pound thinly sliced deli turkey breast
4	fresh strawberries, sliced
2	tablespoons reduced-fat spreadable cream cheese
2	teaspoons finely chopped pecans

On two slices of bread, layer the lettuce, cheese, turkey and strawberries. Combine cream cheese and pecans; spread over remaining bread. Place over strawberries. **Yield: 2 servings.**

Mediterranean Chicken Sandwiches

Marcia Fuller ✳ SHERIDAN, MONTANA

I copied this delightful recipe when I was in Italy visiting my aunt. The refreshing sandwich filling is nicely flavored with oregano and mint. I like it tucked into chewy pita bread.

USES LESS FAT, SUGAR OR SALT. INCLUDES NUTRITION FACTS.

1-1/4	pounds boneless skinless chicken breasts, cut into 1-inch strips
2	medium tomatoes, seeded and chopped
1/2	cup sliced quartered seeded cucumber
1/2	cup sliced sweet onion
2	tablespoons cider vinegar
1	tablespoon olive oil
1	tablespoon minced fresh oregano *or* 1 teaspoon dried oregano
1	to 2 teaspoons minced fresh mint *or* 1/2 teaspoon dried mint
1/4	teaspoon salt
3	whole wheat pita breads, halved, warmed
6	lettuce leaves

In a large nonstick skillet coated with nonstick cooking spray, cook chicken for 5 minutes or until no longer pink. Remove from the skillet; cool slightly.

In a bowl, combine chicken, tomatoes, cucumber and onion. In a jar with a tight-fitting lid, combine the vinegar, oil, oregano, mint and salt; shake well. Pour over chicken mixture; toss gently. Cover and refrigerate for at least 1 hour. Line pita halves with lettuce; fill with chicken mixture, using a slotted spoon. **Yield: 6 servings.**

NUTRITION FACTS: 1 filled pita half equals 227 calories, 4 g fat (1 g saturated fat), 55 mg cholesterol, 335 mg sodium, 22 g carbohydrate, 3 g fiber, 26 g protein.

Mediterranean Chicken Sandwiches

Roast Beef Sandwich Supreme

June Formanek ✳ BELLE PLAINE, IOWA

A tasty, five-ingredient spread adds great flavor to roast beef. We made these many Sunday evenings when we wanted a simple supper. Add a beverage and light dessert for an easy meal.

1/2	cup sour cream
1	tablespoon dry onion soup mix
2	teaspoons prepared horseradish, drained
1/8	teaspoon salt
1/8	teaspoon pepper
12	slices rye bread *or* pumpernickel bread
1	pound sliced deli roast beef (about 12 slices)
6	lettuce leaves

In a small bowl, combine the sour cream, soup mix, horseradish, salt and pepper. Spread over six slices of bread; layer with beef, lettuce and remaining bread. **Yield: 6 servings.**

Nutty Ham and Apple Sandwiches

Dorothy Kirkonij ✳ SOUTH FRANCISCO, CALIFORNIA

Almonds and apple add a pleasant crunch to these out-of-the-ordinary sandwiches. For a little variety, try substituting a different kind of bread or cheese.

Nutty Ham and Apple Sandwiches

Corned Beef and Cabbage Sandwiches

8	teaspoons spicy brown mustard
8	slices rye bread
4	lettuce leaves
1	large tomato, thinly sliced
4	slices cheddar cheese
1/2	pound fully cooked ham, thinly sliced
1	tart apple, thinly sliced
1/4	cup sliced almonds

Spread mustard on each slice of bread. On four slices, layer the lettuce, tomato, cheese, ham and apple. Top with almonds and remaining bread. **Yield: 4 servings.**

Corned Beef and Cabbage Sandwiches

Taste of Home Test Kitchen ✳ GREENDALE, WISCONSIN

You don't have to wait for St. Patrick's Day to serve these festive specialties. Your family is sure to enjoy the creamy cabbage and tender corned beef piled high on a kaiser roll.

1/3	cup mayonnaise
1	tablespoon white vinegar
1/4	teaspoon ground mustard
1/4	teaspoon celery seed
1/4	teaspoon pepper
1-1/2	cups thinly shredded raw cabbage
4	kaiser *or* hard rolls, split
3/4	to 1 pound fully cooked corned beef, sliced

In a small bowl, combine the mayonnaise, vinegar, mustard, celery seed and pepper until blended. Stir in cabbage. Spoon cabbage mixture onto the bottom halves of rolls. Cover with corned beef; replace roll tops. **Yield: 4 servings.**

Hearty Ham Sandwiches

Rena Charmasson ✳ WOODWARD, OKLAHOMA

When our granddaughter needed to serve a bite for a gathering after a high-school dance, I created this recipe. Now these sandwiches, served along with bowls of soup, make a nice meal for me and my husband.

- 2 tablespoons mayonnaise
- 1 tablespoon prepared horseradish
- 1 tablespoon prepared mustard
- 1 tablespoon chopped onion
- 8 slices rye *or* sourdough bread
- 8 thin slices fully cooked ham
- 4 slices Swiss cheese

In a small bowl, combine the mayonnaise, horseradish, mustard and onion. Spread on four slices of bread. Layer with ham and cheese; top with remaining bread. **Yield: 4 servings.**

Chicken Salad Clubs

Sarah Smith ✳ EDGEWOOD, KENTUCKY

Mondays have always been soup-and-sandwich night at our house. One evening, I embellished a regular chicken salad sandwich with some not-so-usual ingredients, like rye bread and honey-mustard dressing. The results were simply outstanding.

- 8 bacon strips
- 4 lettuce leaves
- 8 slices rye *or* pumpernickel bread
- 1 pound prepared chicken salad

Guacamole Turkey Subs

- 4 slices Swiss cheese
- 8 slices tomato
- 1/3 cup honey mustard salad dressing

In a large skillet, cook bacon over medium heat until crisp. Remove to paper towels to drain. Place lettuce on four slices of bread; layer each with chicken salad, two bacon strips, one cheese slice and two tomato slices. Spread salad dressing on one side of remaining bread; place over tomatoes. **Yield: 4 servings.**

Guacamole Turkey Subs

Marci McDonald ✳ AMARILLO, TEXAS

This may sound like a strange combination, but it is without a doubt the best lunch you'll ever eat! I'm always asked for the recipe.

- 1 package (3 ounces) cream cheese, softened
- 1/3 cup prepared guacamole
- 1/4 cup picante sauce
- 3 submarine sandwich buns (about 8 inches), split
- 1-1/2 cups shredded lettuce
- 1 medium tomato, thinly sliced
- 9 slices smoked deli turkey
- 9 bacon strips, cooked and drained

In a large bowl, combine the cream cheese, guacamole and picante sauce; spread over the cut side of the buns.

On bun bottoms, layer half of the lettuce, all of the tomato, turkey and bacon, then remaining lettuce. Replace tops. Cut sandwiches in half; wrap in plastic wrap. Refrigerate until serving. **Yield: 6 servings.**

Chicken Salad Clubs

Turkey Dill Subs

Turkey Dill Subs

Violet Beard ✳ MARSHALL, ILLINOIS

For a change of pace from usual picnic fare, try these dill-seasoned subs. You can use salmon or pickled herring tidbits instead of turkey to make a Swedish hero.

1/2	cup butter, softened
4	tablespoons snipped fresh dill *or* 4 teaspoons dill weed
8	submarine buns (about 8 inches *each*), split

Lettuce leaves

12	radishes, thinly sliced
2	cups thinly sliced zucchini *or* cucumber
2	to 3 teaspoons cider vinegar, optional
2	to 3 pounds thinly sliced deli smoked turkey

In a small bowl, combine butter and dill; spread on sub buns. Layer the lettuce, radishes and zucchini on bottom of buns. Sprinkle with vinegar if desired. Top with turkey; replace bun tops. **Yield: 8 servings.**

Tarragon Chicken Salad Sandwiches

Caroleah Johnson ✳ BERRY CREEK, CALIFORNIA

I became tired of traditional chicken sandwiches, so I came up with this recipe. Tarragon provides a nice subtle seasoning, while sunflower kernels add extra crunch.

1/2	cup mayonnaise
1	tablespoon lemon juice
1	teaspoon Dijon mustard
3	cups cubed cooked chicken
3/4	cup chopped celery
1	tablespoon minced fresh tarragon *or* 1 teaspoon dried tarragon
1/3	cup sunflower kernels
8	croissants *or* rolls, split

Lettuce leaves

In a large bowl, combine the first three ingredients. Stir in chicken, celery and tarragon. Just before serving, add sunflower kernels. Line croissants with lettuce leaves; top lettuce with 1/2 cup chicken salad. **Yield: 8 servings.**

Seafood Salad Sandwiches

Saundra Woods ✳ WOODBURY, TENNESSEE

I've enjoyed cooking for many years...luckily my husband and two sons always anticipated my experiments. Now I have three grandsons who love to eat bites like this at Grandma's house.

USES LESS FAT, SUGAR OR SALT. INCLUDES NUTRITION FACTS.

8	ounces frozen cooked salad shrimp, thawed *or* frozen crabmeat, thawed
3/4	cup chopped celery
1/3	cup mayonnaise
1	teaspoon dried minced onion
1/2	teaspoon dried tarragon, crushed
1/2	teaspoon hot pepper sauce
4	sandwich buns, split

Fresh spinach leaves

In a large bowl, combine the first six ingredients. Cover and chill for at least 1 hour. Spoon 1/2 cup of seafood mixture onto each bun; top with spinach leaves. **Yield: 4 servings.**

NUTRITION FACTS: 1/4 recipe (prepared with shrimp and fat-free mayonnaise) equals 201 calories, 3 g fat (0 saturated fat), 111 mg cholesterol, 673 mg sodium, 26 g carbohydrate, 0 fiber, 15 g protein.

Super Sandwich

Patrice Barker ✳ TAMPA, FLORIDA

This big, meaty crowd-pleaser is one I've made many times when I knew I'd be feeding a hungry bunch. Everyone remarks on the tasty olive salad tucked between the slices of meat and cheese. Since it can be made ahead, you're free to visit with family and friends.

1	medium cucumber, peeled, seeded and chopped

Super Sandwich

1 medium tomato, seeded and chopped
1 small onion, chopped
1/2 cup pitted ripe olives, chopped
1/2 cup pimiento-stuffed olives, chopped
1/4 cup prepared Italian salad dressing
1 round loaf (1-1/2 pounds) unsliced sourdough, white *or* whole wheat bread
1/2 pound sliced fully cooked ham
1/4 pound sliced salami
1/4 pound sliced cooked pork
1/2 pound sliced Swiss cheese
1/2 pound sliced Muenster cheese

In a large bowl, combine cucumber, tomato, onion, olives and salad dressing; set aside.

Cut 1 in. off the top of the bread; set aside. Carefully hollow out top and bottom of loaf, leaving a 1/2-in. shell. (Discard removed bread or save for another use.)

Layer a fourth of the ham, salami, pork and cheeses inside the shell. Top with third of the vegetable mixture. Repeat layers, ending with meat and cheeses, gently pressing down to flatten as needed.

Replace bread top; wrap tightly in plastic. Refrigerate until serving. **Yield: 8 servings.**

easy ALFRESCO

The Super Sandwich is perfect for outdoor get-togethers such as tailgates and picnics. Simply pack a bag of chips, some deli salad and brownies from the bakery for a no-fuss menu. Don't forget a serrated knife to slice the sandwich!

Salmon Dill Croissants

Maya Whittier ✳ ORLEANS, ONTARIO

The original recipe made a cheese ball that my parents only served at Christmas parties. It was so delicious on crackers that I decided to try it as a filling inside croissants. These smoky salmon sandwiches taste so wonderfully rich that everyone assumes they're gourmet.

1 package (8 ounces) cream cheese, softened
1 can (7-1/2 ounces) salmon, drained, bones and skin removed
1/4 cup mayonnaise
1 tablespoon lemon juice
1 tablespoon grated onion
1 teaspoon prepared horseradish
1/2 teaspoon dill weed
1/4 teaspoon salt
1/4 teaspoon garlic powder
1/4 teaspoon Liquid Smoke, optional
6 croissants, split
1 cup shredded lettuce

In a large mixing bowl, beat cream cheese until smooth. Stir in the salmon, mayonnaise, lemon juice, onion, horseradish, dill, salt, garlic powder and Liquid Smoke if desired. Spread over croissants; top with lettuce. **Yield: 6 servings.**

Salmon Dill Croissants

Beef 'n' Olive Sandwiches

Iola Egle ✳ BELLA VISTA, ARKANSAS

To create this rich and creamy sandwich filling, I blend dried beef, olives and walnuts. Cut into quarters, these wedges are sophisticated enough to serve at parties, plus they freeze beautifully for make-ahead convenience.

- 1 package (8 ounces) cream cheese, softened
- 2 tablespoons heavy whipping cream
- 1/2 teaspoon white pepper
- 1/4 cup chopped dried beef
- 3 tablespoons sliced pimiento-stuffed olives
- 3 tablespoons chopped walnuts
- 8 slices bread

In a large mixing bowl, beat the cream cheese, cream and pepper until smooth. Stir in beef, olives and walnuts.

Spread on four slices of bread; top with remaining bread. Cover and freeze for up to 2 months. Remove from the freezer at least 4 hours before serving. Sandwiches may be frozen for up to 3 months. **Yield: 4 servings.**

Home Run Hoagies

Taste of Home Test Kitchen ✳ GREENDALE, WISCONSIN

Kids can pitch in with assembling these colorful subs stacked with chicken, cheese, lettuce and tomatoes. To score with big appetites, try adding extra slices of meat or offer a few varieties of sliced cheese.

Home Run Hoagies

Triple-Decker Salmon Club

- 3/4 cup mayonnaise
- 1/2 cup Italian salad dressing
- 12 hoagie buns, split
- 24 slices thinly sliced deli chicken (about 2-1/2 pounds)
- 12 slices cheddar cheese, halved
- 12 lettuce leaves
- 8 medium tomatoes, sliced

In a small bowl, combine mayonnaise and salad dressing. Spread on cut side of buns. On bun bottoms, layer chicken, cheese, lettuce and tomatoes. Replace bun tops. **Yield: 12 servings.**

Triple-Decker Salmon Club

Jane Bone ✳ CAPE CORAL, FLORIDA

You're in for a tasty treat with my deliciously different triple-deckers. My guests love them... even those who don't ordinarily like salmon or cottage cheese.

- 3/4 cup 4% cottage cheese
- 1/4 cup dill pickle relish
- 1 can (6 ounces) salmon, drained, bones and skin removed
- 1 celery rib, chopped
- 6 slices bread, toasted
- 2 lettuce leaves, optional

In a small bowl, combine cottage cheese and pickle relish. In another bowl, combine salmon and celery. For each sandwich, top one piece of toast with lettuce if desired and half of the cottage cheese mixture. Top with a second piece of toast; spread with half of the salmon mixture. Top with a third piece of toast. **Yield: 2 servings.**

Egg Salad-Cucumber Sandwiches

Lucy Meyring ✳ WALDEN, COLORADO

This is a tasty variation of traditional egg salad. The cucumbers and onion add a refreshing crunch I truly enjoy.

3	hard-cooked eggs, chopped
1/2	cup chopped green pepper
1/4	cup mayonnaise
2	tablespoons chopped red onion
1/2	teaspoon lemon juice
1/8	teaspoon salt
1/8	teaspoon pepper
8	slices whole wheat bread
1	small cucumber, thinly sliced
4	lettuce leaves

In a small bowl, combine the eggs, green pepper, mayonnaise, onion, lemon juice, salt and pepper. Spread mixture on four slices of bread. Top with cucumber and lettuce. Top with remaining bread. **Yield: 4 servings.**

Turkey Tomato Club

Lisa Klicker ✳ WALLA WALLA, WASHINGTON

This stuffed loaf gets its irresistible flavor from a quick-and-easy coleslaw. You'll never make an ordinary club again.

1/2	cup mayonnaise
1	tablespoon cider vinegar
2	teaspoons sugar
1/4	teaspoon salt
1/8	teaspoon pepper
4	cups thinly sliced cabbage
1	round loaf sourdough bread (1 pound)
10	bacon strips, cooked and drained
6	slices tomato
1	cup thinly sliced cucumber
1/2	pound thinly sliced smoked turkey

In a large bowl, combine the first five ingredients. Add cabbage; toss to coat. Cover and refrigerate for 30 minutes.

Cut a thin slice off the top of the bread; hollow out bottom half, leaving a 1-in. shell. (Discard removed bread or save for another use.) Place half of the cabbage mixture in bottom of loaf. Layer with the bacon, tomato, cucumber and turkey; top with remaining cabbage mixture. Replace bread top. Cut into wedges. **Yield: 6-8 servings.**

Sourdough Veggie Sandwiches

Billie Moss ✳ WALNUT CREEK, CALIFORNIA

These appealing delights are a snap to assemble. We love them after church on Sundays.

2	tablespoons mayonnaise
4	slices sourdough bread
1	cup (4 ounces) shredded cheddar cheese
2	small zucchini, halved lengthwise
1	large tomato, thinly sliced
1/4	cup shredded carrot
1	to 2 tablespoons salted sunflower kernels
2	tablespoons butter, softened

Spread mayonnaise on one side of each slice of bread. On two slices, layer the cheese, zucchini, tomato, carrot and sunflower kernels. Top with remaining bread, mayonnaise side down. Spread butter over the outside of bread.

In a large skillet, cook over medium heat until bread is lightly toasted and cheese is melted. **Yield: 2 servings.**

Sourdough Veggie Sandwiches

4 green salads

Crisp and refreshing, a good green salad is hard to beat. And these colorful, flavor-packed sensations are sure to make your mouth water. Get creative by topping your salad with sliced fruit, make it an entree by adding chicken or beef, or savor the simplicity of a salad chock-full of garden veggies.

page 51

page 57

page 48

Sesame Chicken Over Greens

Sesame Chicken Over Greens

Diana Mullins ✳ LEXINGTON, KENTUCKY

My teenage sons can't get enough of this dish... and I like it, too. The grilled chicken strips make the salad hearty enough for a meal, but the assorted veggies keep it nice and light.

1/4	cup reduced-sodium teriyaki sauce
2	tablespoons red wine vinegar
2	tablespoons canola oil
2	tablespoons honey
2	teaspoons crushed red pepper flakes
1	garlic clove, minced
4	boneless skinless chicken breast halves (1 pound)
5	cups torn mixed salad greens
1/2	cup sliced sweet red pepper
1/2	cup shredded carrot
4	green onions, sliced
1	can (2-1/4 ounces) sliced ripe olives, drained
1/2	cup ranch salad dressing
1	tablespoon sesame seeds, toasted

In a large resealable plastic bag, combine the first six ingredients. Add chicken; seal bag and turn to coat. Refrigerate for several hours or overnight.

Drain and discard marinade. Grill chicken, uncovered, over medium heat for 5-7 minutes on each side or until juices run clear.

On four serving plates, divide the greens, red pepper, carrot, onions and olives. Thinly slice chicken and arrange over salad. Drizzle with ranch dressing; sprinkle with sesame seeds. **Yield: 4 servings.**

Beet Spinach Salad

Marguerite Shaeffer ✳ SEWELL, NEW JERSEY

This salad bursts with fresh flavors, making it a surefire winner with anyone who tries it. After one bite, people are sure to ask for the recipe.

2	large fresh beets
2	tablespoons red wine vinegar
1	teaspoon Dijon mustard
1/4	cup olive oil
1-1/2	teaspoons sugar
1/8	teaspoon salt

Dash pepper

1/2	cup chopped green onions
1/2	teaspoon minced fresh mint
4	cups torn fresh spinach
1	medium navel orange, peeled and sectioned
1/2	cup fresh raspberries

Place beets in a large saucepan and cover with water. Bring to a boil. Reduce heat; cover and simmer for 30 minutes or until tender. Cool; peel and cut into 1/4-in. strips.

In a small bowl, whisk vinegar and mustard until blended; gradually whisk in oil. Add the sugar, salt and pepper. In a large bowl, combine the beets, onions, mint and 2 tablespoons vinaigrette. Cover and refrigerate for 30 minutes.

In a large salad bowl, combine the spinach, orange sections, beet mixture and remaining vinaigrette; toss. Top salad with raspberries and serve immediately. **Yield: 4 servings.**

Beet Spinach Salad

Bacon-Swiss Tossed Salad

Bacon-Swiss Tossed Salad

Cathee Bethel ✳ PHILOMATH, OREGON

This favorite came from a cookbook compiled by the women of the church in my hometown of Chico, California. The salad is pretty and tasty. But best of all, it can be put together a couple of hours before serving. When it's time, simply toss and it's ready.

1/2	cup mayonnaise
1	tablespoon sugar
1/4	teaspoon salt
1/4	teaspoon pepper
6	cups torn mixed salad greens
1	medium red onion, sliced
1	package (10 ounces) frozen peas, thawed
8	ounces sliced Swiss cheese, julienned
1	pound bacon, cooked and crumbled

In a small bowl, combine mayonnaise, sugar, salt and pepper. In a large salad bowl, layer a third of the greens and a third of the mayonnaise mixture, onion, peas and Swiss cheese. Repeat the layers twice. Cover and refrigerate for at least 2 hours. Just before serving, add the crumbled bacon and toss. **Yield: 6-8 servings.**

better BACON

When a recipe calls for bacon bits (for sprinkling over a salad, etc.), use your kitchen scissors to cut uncooked bacon into small pieces. Fry in a skillet, stirring often as the bacon cooks. Then drain and pat dry on a paper towel.

Chicken Pear Mixed Greens Salad

Janet Duran ✳ DES MOINES, WASHINGTON

Homemade vinaigrette pairs well with the grilled chicken, juicy pears and Brie cheese that star in this satisfying entree salad.

USES LESS FAT, SUGAR OR SALT. INCLUDES NUTRITION FACTS.

5	boneless skinless chicken breast halves (4 ounces *each*)
7	cups torn mixed salad greens
2	ounces Brie *or* Camembert cheese, cubed
2	medium pears, chopped
1/4	cup chopped pecans, toasted
1/4	cup apple juice concentrate, thawed
2	tablespoons canola oil
4-1/2	teaspoons cider vinegar
2	teaspoons Dijon mustard
1/4	teaspoon salt
1/8	teaspoon pepper

Coat grill rack with nonstick cooking spray before starting the grill. Grill chicken, covered, over medium heat for 6-8 minutes on each side or until juices run clear.

Arrange the salad greens, cheese, pears and pecans on individual plates. Slice chicken; arrange over salad. In a jar with a tight-fitting lid, combine the apple juice concentrate, oil, vinegar, mustard, salt and pepper; shake well. Drizzle over salad and serve immediately. **Yield: 5 servings.**

NUTRITION FACTS: 1 serving equals 329 calories, 16 g fat (4 g saturated fat), 74 mg cholesterol, 317 mg sodium, 19 g carbohydrate, 4 g fiber, 27 g protein.

Chicken Pear Mixed Greens Salad

Guacamole Salad Bowl

Ann Eastman ✳ GREENVILLE, CALIFORNIA

The bowl is usually "licked clean" when I make this hearty dish for our group. I sometimes substitute tuna for the shrimp.

- 5 cups torn leaf lettuce
- 2 medium tomatoes, cut into wedges
- 1 cup (4 ounces) shredded cheddar cheese
- 1 cup cooked salad shrimp
- 1 cup corn chips
- 1/2 cup sliced ripe olives
- 1/4 cup sliced green onions

AVOCADO DRESSING:

- 1/2 cup mashed ripe avocado
- 1 tablespoon lemon juice
- 1/2 cup sour cream
- 1/3 cup vegetable oil
- 1 garlic clove, minced
- 1/2 teaspoon sugar
- 1/2 teaspoon chili powder
- 1/4 teaspoon salt
- 1/4 teaspoon hot pepper sauce

In a large salad bowl, combine the first seven ingredients; set aside. In a blender, combine dressing ingredients; cover and process until smooth. Pour over salad; toss to coat. Serve immediately. **Yield: 6-8 servings.**

Crunchy Tossed Salad With Chicken

Ileene Nodland ✳ DUNN CENTER, NORTH DAKOTA

I like to prepare this in the summer when the men are late getting in from the fields. Chicken and a zesty dressing turn simple greens into a satisfying main meal.

- 6 cups torn lettuce
- 3 cups cubed cooked chicken
- 1 cup sliced celery
- 1 cup shredded carrots
- 1/4 cup sliced green onions
- 3/4 cup mayonnaise
- 1/4 cup milk
- 2 tablespoons tarragon vinegar
- 3 to 4 teaspoons prepared mustard

Submarine Sandwich Salad

- 1/2 teaspoon pepper
- 2 cups potato sticks

In a large bowl, combine the lettuce, chicken, celery, carrots and onions. In a small bowl, whisk the mayonnaise, milk, vinegar, mustard and pepper. Pour over salad; lightly toss to coat. Add potato sticks; serve immediately. **Yield: 4-6 servings.**

Submarine Sandwich Salad

Julie Vogl ✳ CUMBERLAND, IOWA

If your family's like mine, they won't be able to resist this salad loaded with meat, produce...even bread! The recipe can easily be doubled, so I often serve it at potlucks.

- 5 to 6 cups torn lettuce
- 1 to 2 hard rolls, cubed
- 1 medium tomato, chopped
- 1/2 cup thinly sliced red onion
- 1/2 cup shredded Swiss cheese
- 2 ounces *each* ham, turkey and salami, julienned
- 1/2 cup sliced pepperoni

DRESSING:

- 1/3 cup vegetable oil
- 2 tablespoons tarragon vinegar
- 1/4 to 1/2 teaspoon dried oregano
- 1/4 teaspoon salt
- 1/8 teaspoon garlic powder

Dash pepper

In a large salad bowl, combine the lettuce, rolls, tomato, onion, cheese, ham, turkey, salami and pepperoni. In a jar with a tight-fitting lid, combine the dressing ingredients; shake well. Drizzle over salad; toss to coat. **Yield: 6 servings.**

Beef Tenderloin Salad

Taste of Home Test Kitchen ✳ GREENDALE, WISCONSIN

Slices of tender beef tenderloin, fresh asparagus and juicy tomatoes star in this attractive entree salad. Try serving it with a loaf of warm, chewy French bread.

USES LESS FAT, SUGAR OR SALT. INCLUDES NUTRITION FACTS.

1/4	cup fat-free mayonnaise
2	tablespoons Dijon mustard
1	tablespoon fat-free milk
2	teaspoons white vinegar
1	teaspoon prepared horseradish
1-1/4	teaspoons sugar
3/8	teaspoon salt, *divided*
1/4	teaspoon pepper, *divided*
8	cups water
1	pound fresh asparagus, trimmed, cut into 2-inch pieces
4	beef tenderloin steaks (4 ounces *each*)
1	large garlic clove, peeled and halved
6	cups torn mixed salad greens
2	large ripe tomatoes, cut into wedges

In a small bowl, whisk the mayonnaise, mustard, milk, vinegar, horseradish, sugar, 1/8 teaspoon salt and 1/8 teaspoon pepper. Cover and refrigerate.

In a large saucepan, bring water to a boil. Add asparagus; cover and boil for 3 minutes. Drain and immediately place asparagus in ice water. Drain and pat dry. Cover and refrigerate.

If grilling the steaks, coat grill rack with nonstick cooking spray before starting the grill. Rub steaks

Beef Tenderloin Salad

with garlic; discard garlic. Sprinkle with remaining salt and pepper.

Grill steaks, covered, over medium heat or broil 4-6 in. from the heat for 6-8 minutes on each side or until meat reaches desired doneness (for medium-rare, a meat thermometer should read 145°; medium, 160°; well-done, 170°).

On four serving plates, arrange the greens, tomatoes and asparagus. Thinly slice beef; place over salad. Drizzle with dressing. **Yield: 4 servings.**

NUTRITION FACTS: 1 serving equals 259 calories, 10 g fat (3 g saturated fat), 14 mg cholesterol, 610 mg sodium, 14 g carbohydrate, 4 g fiber, 29 g protein.

Baby Corn Romaine Salad

Kathryn Maxson ✳ MOUNTLAKE TERRACE, WASHINGTON

My kids really enjoy this crisp combination, made with romaine lettuce, broccoli, corn and crumbled bacon. It uses bottled dressing, so it's quick to fix, too.

USES LESS FAT, SUGAR OR SALT. INCLUDES NUTRITION FACTS.

6	cups torn romaine
2	cups fresh broccoli florets
1	can (15 ounces) whole baby corn, rinsed, drained and cut into 1/2-inch pieces
3	tablespoons crumbled cooked bacon
1/2	cup fat-free Caesar *or* Italian salad dressing

In a large salad bowl, combine the romaine, broccoli, corn and bacon. Drizzle with dressing; toss to coat. **Yield: 6 servings.**

NUTRITION FACTS: 1 cup equals 43 calories, 2 g fat (1 g saturated fat), 3 mg cholesterol, 329 mg sodium, 4 g carbohydrate, 2 g fiber, 3 g protein.

Baby Corn Romaine Salad

Black Bean Chicken Salad

Black Bean Chicken Salad

Jean Ecos ✳ HARTLAND, WISCONSIN

A refreshing mix of chicken, black beans and crisp garden veggies is tossed with a light lime vinaigrette. This satisfying salad is sure to be a winner on hot summer days! I like to serve it with tortilla chips and salsa.

6	cups torn lettuce
1-1/2	cups cubed cooked chicken breast
1	can (15 ounces) black beans, rinsed and drained
1	cup chopped seeded tomatoes
1	cup chopped green pepper
1/2	cup sliced red onion
1/2	cup shredded cheddar cheese

LIME VINAIGRETTE:

1/4	cup minced fresh cilantro
1/4	cup chopped seeded tomato
1	tablespoon cider vinegar
1	tablespoon olive oil
1	tablespoon lime juice
1/2	teaspoon grated lime peel
1	garlic clove, minced
1/4	teaspoon salt
1/4	teaspoon pepper
1/4	teaspoon chili powder

In a large serving bowl, combine the torn lettuce, chicken, black beans, tomatoes, green pepper, onion and cheddar cheese. In a blender or food processor, combine the vinaigrette ingredients; cover and process until smooth. Pour dressing over salad and toss to coat. **Yield: 4 servings.**

Hot Bacon Asparagus Salad

Paulette Balda ✳ PROPHETSTOWN, ILLINOIS

This meal-in-one salad is so easy to fix when I get home from work...but it looks like I spent an hour preparing it. It's great with warm rolls.

7	bacon strips, diced
1	pound fresh asparagus, trimmed
1/3	cup white vinegar
1	tablespoon sugar
1/2	teaspoon ground mustard
1/4	teaspoon pepper
4	cups torn salad greens
1/2	cup sliced almonds
2	hard-cooked eggs, sliced

In a large skillet, cook bacon over medium heat until crisp. Using a slotted spoon, remove to paper towels to drain, reserving 2-3 tablespoons drippings. Cut asparagus into 1-1/2-in. pieces; saute in drippings until crisp-tender. Add the vinegar, sugar, mustard, pepper and bacon. Cook and stir for 1-2 minutes or until heated through.

In a large salad bowl, combine salad greens and almonds. Add the asparagus mixture; toss gently. Arrange egg over the salad and serve immediately. **Yield: 6 servings.**

Fruity Green Salad

Hope Ralph ✳ WOBURN, MASSACHUSETTS

Jazz up traditional greens with juicy pear slices, dried cherries and a delicious dressing that features a touch of honey.

USES LESS FAT, SUGAR OR SALT. INCLUDES NUTRITION FACTS.

Fruity Green Salad

Hot Bacon Asparagus Salad

1 package (5 ounces) salad greens
2/3 cup dried cranberries
1 medium ripe pear, peeled and cubed
3/4 cup seasoned croutons
2 tablespoons sunflower kernels
1/4 cup Italian salad dressing

In a large salad bowl, combine the salad greens, cranberries, pear, croutons and sunflower kernels. Just before serving, add the dressing and toss to coat. **Yield: 6 servings.**

NUTRITION FACTS: 1 cup equals 137 calories, 6 g fat (1 g saturated fat), trace cholesterol, 253 mg sodium, 20 g carbohydrate, 2 g fiber, 2 g protein.

6 cups torn mixed salad greens *or* 1 package (10 ounces) fresh spinach, torn
2 medium ripe pears, thinly sliced
1/3 cup dried cherries *or* cranberries
1/4 cup balsamic vinegar
2 tablespoons honey, warmed
1/4 teaspoon salt
1/8 teaspoon pepper

In a salad bowl, toss the greens, pears and cherries. In a small bowl, combine the vinegar, honey, salt and pepper. Drizzle over salad and toss to coat. Serve immediately. **Yield: 4 servings.**

NUTRITION FACTS: 1-1/2 cups equals 134 calories, 1 g fat (trace saturated fat), 0 cholesterol, 170 mg sodium, 32 g carbohydrate, 5 g fiber, 2 g protein.

Cranberry Tossed Salad

Janelle Halbert ✳ CALGARY, ALBERTA

Tart cranberries and sweet pears make an outstanding duo in this sure-to-please dish. I like topping it with a sprinkling of sunflower kernels for a satisfying crunch.

USES LESS FAT, SUGAR OR SALT. INCLUDES NUTRITION FACTS.

Artichoke Tossed Salad

Melissa Mosness ✳ LOVELAND, COLORADO

I used to care for an elderly woman who loved artichokes, so I created this salad especially for her. Not only is it convenient to make, but you can dress it up with salad shrimp, too.

2 cups *each* torn romaine, leaf and iceberg lettuce
1 jar (6-1/2 ounces) marinated artichoke hearts, drained and chopped
1 cup sliced fresh mushrooms
1 can (2-1/4 ounces) sliced ripe olives, drained
1/2 cup Italian salad dressing

In a salad bowl, combine the greens, artichokes, mushrooms and olives. Drizzle with salad dressing; toss to coat. Serve immediately. **Yield: 6 servings.**

Artichoke Tossed Salad

perfect PEARS

Purchase pears that are firm, fragrant and free of blemishes or soft spots. To ripen pears, place them in a paper bag at room temperature for several days. To prevent pear slices from discoloring, toss with a little lemon juice.

Buffalo Steak Salad

Burt Guenin ✳ CHAPPELL, NEBRASKA

We raise buffalo on our ranch, so I cook plenty of buffalo steak as well as other cuts. During the warmer months, this recipe is a refreshing change of pace from heavier meals. The meat is tender and the dressing is mouth-watering.

1/3	cup olive oil
2	tablespoons red wine vinegar
1	tablespoon lemon juice
1	garlic clove, minced
1/2	teaspoon salt
1/8	teaspoon pepper

Dash Worcestershire sauce

1/2	cup crumbled blue cheese
2	buffalo sirloin *or* rib eye steaks (about 8 ounces *each*)
6	cups torn salad greens
1	medium tomato, thinly sliced
1	small carrot, thinly sliced
1/2	cup thinly sliced onion
1/4	cup sliced pimiento-stuffed olives

In a small bowl, combine the first seven ingredients; mix well. Stir in the crumbled blue cheese. Cover and refrigerate.

Grill steaks, uncovered, over medium-hot heat for 6-10 minutes on each side or until meat reaches desired doneness (for medium-rare, a meat thermometer should read 145°; medium, 160°; well-done, 170°). Thinly slice meat.

On a serving platter or individual salad plates, arrange greens, tomato, carrot, onion and olives. Top with steak and dressing. **Yield: 4 servings.**

Buffalo Steak Salad

Hearty Reuben Salad

Hearty Reuben Salad

Mrs. Paul Tremblay ✳ FORT WAYNE, INDIANA

It's the popular Reuben in a salad! All your favorite ingredients from the classic handheld version—sauerkraut, Swiss cheese, corned beef and Thousand Island dressing—star in this satisfying entree salad.

4	cups torn iceberg lettuce
1	can (16 ounces) sauerkraut, rinsed and drained
1	cup cubed Swiss cheese
2	packages (2-1/2 ounces *each*) sliced corned beef, chopped
2	tablespoons chopped fresh parsley
1/4	to 1/2 cup Thousand Island salad dressing
1/2	cup rye croutons
4	hard-cooked eggs, quartered

In a large salad bowl, combine the lettuce, sauerkraut, cheese, corned beef and parsley. Drizzle with dressing; toss to coat. Garnish with croutons and eggs. Serve immediately. **Yield: 4 servings.**

Tomato Spinach Salad

Ruth Seitz ✳ COLUMBUS JUNCTION, IOWA

This recipe is a longtime favorite. When I serve the fresh spinach tossed with a creamy dill dressing, I receive plenty of compliments.

1/2	cup mayonnaise
1/2	cup grated Parmesan cheese
1/4	cup milk
1-1/2	teaspoons dill weed
1-1/2	teaspoons dried minced onion
1-1/2	teaspoons lemon-pepper seasoning

1   package (10 ounces) fresh spinach, torn
2   cups cherry tomatoes

In a jar with tight-fitting lid, combine first six ingredients; shake well. Refrigerate for at least 1 hour. Just before serving, in a large salad bowl, combine spinach and tomatoes. Shake dressing; drizzle over salad and toss. **Yield: 6-8 servings.**

Stuffed Iceberg Wedges

Rosemarie Surwillo ✳ LAKE ST. LOUIS, MISSOURI

Here's a creative spin on the usual green lettuce salad. Wedges of crisp, cold iceberg lettuce are stuffed with a zesty filling. Try pairing the wedges with fresh-baked breadsticks.

1	medium head iceberg lettuce
1/3	cup mayonnaise
1/4	teaspoon curry powder
1	cup (4 ounces) shredded cheddar cheese
1/2	cup coarsely chopped fully cooked ham
1/2	cup chopped celery
1/4	cup minced fresh parsley
1	jar (2 ounces) diced pimientos, drained

Salad dressing of your choice

Remove core from the head of lettuce. Carefully hollow out lettuce, leaving a 3/4-in. shell (save removed lettuce for another use).

In a small bowl, combine the mayonnaise and curry powder. Add the cheese, ham, celery, parsley and pimientos; mix well. Spoon into lettuce shell. Tightly wrap in plastic wrap; refrigerate for at least 3 hours. Cut into wedges. Serve wedges with salad dressing. **Yield: 4-6 servings.**

Stuffed Iceberg Wedges

Watermelon Spinach Salad

Watermelon Spinach Salad

Taste of Home Test Kitchen ✳ GREENDALE, WISCONSIN

Dark green spinach leaves provide a rich backdrop for brilliant raspberries, cubed watermelon and sliced almonds in this eye-appealing salad. The light vinaigrette is the perfect way to dress up summer's finest produce.

POPPY SEED VINAIGRETTE:

1/2	cup white wine vinegar
1/2	cup sugar
1/2	teaspoon ground mustard
1/4	teaspoon onion powder
1/2	teaspoon salt
1/2	cup vegetable oil
1/4	cup chopped onion
1	teaspoon poppy seeds

SALAD:

1	package (6 ounces) fresh baby spinach, torn
2	cups seeded cubed watermelon
1	cup halved green grapes
1	cup fresh raspberries
1/4	cup sliced almonds

In a blender, combine the vinegar, sugar, mustard, onion powder and salt. Cover and process until sugar is dissolved. Continue processing while adding oil in a steady stream. Add onion and poppy seeds; process until blended.

In a large salad bowl, combine the spinach, watermelon, grapes and raspberries; sprinkle with almonds. Serve with vinaigrette. **Yield: 8 servings (about 1 cup vinaigrette).**

Guacamole Tossed Salad

Guacamole Tossed Salad

Lori Fisher ✳ CHINO HILLS, CALIFORNIA

Tomatoes, onion, bacon and avocados dress up salad greens in this rave-winning salad. Tossed in a zesty dressing, it's sure to bring many compliments and recipe requests.

> 2 medium tomatoes, seeded and chopped
> 1/2 small red onion, sliced and separated into rings
>
> Bacon strips, cooked and crumbled
>
> 2 large ripe avocados, peeled and cubed
> 1/3 cup vegetable oil
> 2 tablespoons cider vinegar
> 1 teaspoon salt
> 1/4 teaspoon pepper
> 1/4 teaspoon hot pepper sauce
> 4 cups torn salad greens

In a large salad bowl, combine the tomatoes, onion and bacon; add avocados.

In a small bowl, whisk the oil, cider vinegar, salt, pepper and hot pepper sauce. Pour dressing over tomato mixture and toss gently. Serve immediately. **Yield: 4 servings.**

Make-Ahead Meatball Salad

Rexann LaFleur ✳ TWIN FALLS, IDAHO

I must admit when my husband's grandma served this, we were all a little leery. But the first bite was very convincing...and then we couldn't get enough of the tasty salad.

> 1 pound ground beef
> 1/2 cup seasoned bread crumbs
> 1/2 cup Italian salad dressing
> 6 cups torn salad greens
> 1 medium red onion, thinly sliced
> 1 cup (4 ounces) shredded part-skim mozzarella cheese
> 1 can (2-1/4 ounces) sliced ripe olives, drained
>
> Caesar Italian salad dressing *or* dressing of your choice

In a large bowl, combine beef and bread crumbs. Shape into 3/4-in. balls. Place meatballs on a greased rack in a shallow baking pan. Bake at 350° for 15-20 minutes or until meat is no longer pink; drain. Cool for 15-30 minutes.

Place Italian salad dressing in a resealable plastic bag; add meatballs. Seal and refrigerate overnight. Drain and discard marinade.

On a serving platter or individual plates, arrange the salad greens, onion, cheese and olives. Top with meatballs. Drizzle with dressing. **Yield: 4 servings.**

Chinese Chicken Salad

Sandra Miller ✳ LEXINGTON, KENTUCKY

This Asian-inspired specialty has a slightly tangy taste and is a refreshing alternative to the typical chicken salad. An added plus is that it is easy to prepare. My favorite way to serve this dish is with fresh fruit and a muffin.

> 3 cups cubed cooked chicken breast
> 3 celery ribs, chopped
> 1 cup canned bean sprouts, rinsed and drained
> 1/2 cup French salad dressing
> 1/2 cup mayonnaise
> 2 tablespoons reduced-sodium soy sauce
> 1/4 teaspoon onion powder
> 1/4 teaspoon salt
> 1/8 teaspoon pepper
> 1/8 teaspoon Chinese five-spice powder
> 5 cups torn salad greens
> 2 tablespoons sliced ripe olives

In a large bowl, combine the first 10 ingredients; toss to coat. Cover and refrigerate for at least 2 hours. Serve chicken mixture on salad greens; garnish with olives. **Yield: 5 servings.**

Honey-Pecan Kiwi Salad

Walnut-Cheese Spinach Salad

Christine Wilson ✳ SELLERSVILLE, PENNSYLVANIA

Tangy, homemade raspberry vinaigrette dressing gives a summery flavor and a pretty pink-red tint to this favorite. It's one salad that's special enough to serve to company.

2	cups fresh raspberries
1/3	cup sugar
1/3	cup vegetable oil
2	tablespoons white vinegar
1/4	teaspoon Worcestershire sauce, optional
1	package (6 ounces) fresh baby spinach
1	small red onion, thinly sliced and separated into rings
1/2	to 1 cup crumbled feta cheese
1/2	cup chopped walnuts

In a saucepan, combine raspberries and sugar; bring to a boil over medium heat. Cook for 1 minute. Strain and discard pulp. In a blender, combine the raspberry juice, vegetable oil, white vinegar and Worcestershire sauce if desired; cover and process until smooth.

In a large salad bowl, combine the spinach, onion, cheese and walnuts. Drizzle with desired amount of dressing; toss to coat. Refrigerate any remaining dressing. **Yield: 8 servings.**

Honey-Pecan Kiwi Salad

Marla Arbet ✳ WHEATLAND, WISCONSIN

This dish won second place in a summer salad recipe feature published in our local newspaper, but it takes first place with my family, who loves to try all my new creations.

USES LESS FAT, SUGAR OR SALT. INCLUDES NUTRITION FACTS.

5	cups torn Boston lettuce
3	kiwifruit, peeled and sliced
1/4	cup chopped pecans, toasted
2	tablespoons vanilla yogurt
2	tablespoons lemon juice
1	tablespoon olive oil
1	tablespoon honey

In a large bowl, combine lettuce, kiwi and pecans. In a small bowl, mix yogurt, lemon juice, oil and honey until smooth. Pour over salad and toss. Serve immediately. **Yield: 4-6 servings.**

NUTRITION FACTS: 3/4 cup equals 100 calories, 6 g fat (1 g saturated fat), 1 mg cholesterol, 8 mg sodium, 11 g carbohydrate, 2 g fiber, 2 g protein.

toasted NUTS

To toast nuts, spread them in a baking pan and bake at 350° until golden brown, stirring often. Generally, nuts will be toasted in 6-10 minutes, but timing will depend on your baking pan and how finely the nuts are chopped.

Walnut-Cheese Spinach Salad

Peanut Chicken Salad

Belinda Gail Brown ✳ WEDOWEE, ALABAMA

Living in Alabama, where lots of peanuts are grown, I've learned to fix many different dishes using this locally raised crop. Here is one of my family's favorites.

1/4	cup sugar
1/4	cup cider vinegar
1-1/2	teaspoons vegetable oil
1/2	teaspoon salt

Dash pepper

4	cups shredded lettuce
2	cups cubed cooked chicken
1	can (15 ounces) mandarin oranges, drained
1	celery rib, thinly sliced
1	green onion, thinly sliced
1	cup chow mein noodles
1/2	cup salted peanuts, toasted

In a jar with a tight-fitting lid, combine the first five ingredients; shake well. In a serving bowl, combine the lettuce, chicken, oranges, celery and onion; stir in chow mein noodles and peanuts. Pour dressing over the salad and toss to coat. Serve immediately. **Yield: 2-4 servings.**

Peanut Chicken Salad

8	cups torn mixed salad greens
1	can (11 ounces) mandarin oranges, drained
1/4	cup coarsely chopped pecans, toasted
1/2	cup peach yogurt
3	tablespoons mayonnaise
1	tablespoon cider vinegar

Divide the salad greens, oranges and pecans among four individual salad plates. In a small bowl, whisk the yogurt, mayonnaise and vinegar; drizzle over salads. **Yield: 4 servings.**

Peachy Pecan Salad

Elissa Armbruster ✳ MEDFORD, NEW JERSEY

The sweet-and-salty combination of mandarin oranges, crunchy pecans and a creamy peach dressing can't be topped! I like to serve this salad with slices of melon.

Peachy Pecan Salad

Apple-Nut Tossed Salad

Maureen Reubelt ✳ GALES FERRY, CONNECTICUT

When you want an alternative to plain greens, give this a try. A light dressing tops crisp apple, walnuts and lettuce sprinkled with blue cheese.

3	tablespoons olive oil
1	teaspoon Dijon mustard
3/4	teaspoon sugar

Salt and pepper to taste

1/2	cup chopped apple
1	tablespoon chopped green onion
3	cups torn Bibb lettuce
1	to 2 tablespoons chopped walnuts
1	to 2 tablespoons crumbled blue cheese

In a large bowl, whisk the oil, mustard, sugar, salt and pepper. Add apple and onion; toss to coat. Add lettuce, walnuts and blue cheese; toss gently. Serve immediately. **Yield: 4 servings.**

Sweet Spinach Salad

Carole Martin ✳ TALLAHASSEE, FLORIDA

This slightly sweet spinach salad is a tasty accompaniment to any meal. Plus, it's quick to fix, so it's on the table in a jiffy.

1	package (10 ounces) fresh spinach, torn
1	can (11 ounces) mandarin oranges, drained
10	cherry tomatoes, halved
1	cup sliced fresh mushrooms

DRESSING:

1/3	cup sugar
3	tablespoons cider vinegar
1	tablespoon honey
1/2	teaspoon dried minced onion
1/2	teaspoon celery seed
1/2	teaspoon ground mustard
1/2	teaspoon paprika
1/2	teaspoon lemon juice
1/2	cup vegetable oil
1	can (2.8 ounces) French-fried onions

In a large salad bowl, toss the spinach, mandarin oranges, tomatoes and mushrooms; set aside. In a microwave-safe bowl, combine the first eight dressing ingredients. Microwave on high for 30-60 seconds. Stir until the sugar is dissolved. Whisk in oil. Drizzle over salad; toss to coat. Sprinkle with onions. **Yield: 6-8 servings.**

EDITOR'S NOTE: This recipe was tested in a 1,100-watt microwave.

Sirloin Caesar Salad

Sirloin Caesar Salad

Carol Sinclair ✳ ST. ELMO, ILLINOIS

A tangy sauce that combines bottled salad dressing, lemon juice and Dijon mustard flavors this filling main-dish salad. You save on cleanup time, too, because both the steak and bread are prepared on the grill.

1	boneless top sirloin steak (1 pound)
1	cup Caesar salad dressing
1/4	cup Dijon mustard
1/4	cup lemon juice
6	slices French bread (1 inch thick)
12	cups torn romaine
1	medium tomato, chopped

Place steak in a large resealable plastic bag or shallow glass container. In a bowl, combine salad dressing, mustard and lemon juice; set aside 3/4 cup. Pour remaining dressing mixture over the steak. Seal or cover and refrigerate for 1 hour, turning occasionally.

Brush both sides of bread with 1/4 cup of the reserved dressing mixture. Grill bread, uncovered, over medium heat for 1-2 minutes on each side or until lightly toasted. Wrap in foil and set aside.

Drain steak, discarding marinade. Grill, covered, for 5-8 minutes on each side or until meat reaches desired doneness (for medium-rare, a meat thermometer should read 145°; medium, 160°; well-done, 170°). Place romaine and tomato on serving platter. Slice steak diagonally; arrange over salad. Serve with the bread and remaining dressing. **Yield: 6 servings.**

Sweet Spinach Salad

5 potatoes, pasta & more

Featuring exciting, new flavors—along with timeless standards—this collection of potato salads, pasta medleys, coleslaws and fruit salads offers an assortment of pleasing sides. Whether you need a dish to pass or just to round out a meal, these fresh combinations do the trick.

page 68

page 64

page 63

Beefy Broccoli Asparagus Salad

Beefy Broccoli Asparagus Salad

Betty Rassette ✳ SALINA, KANSAS

Here's a sensational, lightened-up switch from your everyday dinners. Colorful veggies provide the make-ahead main dish with crispness, while soy sauce and sesame oil add an Asian flair to the homemade dressing.

USES LESS FAT, SUGAR OR SALT. INCLUDES NUTRITION FACTS.

3/4	pound boneless beef sirloin steak
8	cups water
4	cups cut fresh asparagus (1-inch pieces)
2	cups fresh broccoli florets
1/4	cup reduced-sodium soy sauce
2	tablespoons white wine vinegar
4-1/2	teaspoons sesame oil
1	teaspoon minced fresh gingerroot
2	teaspoons sugar

Dash pepper

Place steak on a broiler pan coated with nonstick cooking spray. Broil 3-4 in. from the heat for 6-10 minutes on each side or until meat reaches desired doneness (for medium-rare, a meat thermometer should read 145°; medium, 160°; well-done, 170°); cool completely.

In a large saucepan, bring water to a boil. Add asparagus and broccoli; cover and cook for 3 minutes. Drain and immediately place vegetables in ice water. Drain and pat dry; refrigerate.

For dressing, in a jar with a tight-fitting lid, combine the soy sauce, vinegar, oil, ginger, sugar and pepper; shake well. Thinly slice beef and place in a bowl; add dressing and toss to coat. Cover and refrigerate for 1 hour. Just before serving, add vegetables and toss to coat. **Yield: 4 servings.**

NUTRITION FACTS: One serving (1-1/4 cups) equals 229 calories, 10 g fat (2 g saturated fat), 56 mg cholesterol, 670 mg sodium, 11 g carbohydrate, 3 g fiber, 24 g protein.

Pudding-Topped Fruit Salad

Michelle Masciarelli ✳ TORRINGTON, CONNECTICUT

My sister shared this recipe with me. She served the fruit in wine goblets, topped with the pudding. For large groups, serve the salad in a big bowl. Either way, it's delicious.

USES LESS FAT, SUGAR OR SALT. INCLUDES NUTRITION FACTS.

1	can (20 ounces) pineapple chunks
1	can (8 ounces) crushed pineapple, undrained
1	cup (8 ounces) sour cream
1	package (3.4 ounces) instant vanilla pudding mix
2	medium ripe bananas, sliced
2	cups fresh *or* frozen blueberries, thawed
2	medium ripe peaches, peeled and sliced
2	cups sliced fresh strawberries
1	cup green grapes
1	cup seedless red grapes

Fresh mint, optional

Drain pineapple chunks, reserving juice; refrigerate pineapple. Add water to juice if necessary to measure 3/4 cup. In a large bowl, combine the juice, crushed pineapple, sour cream and pudding mix until blended. Cover and refrigerate for at least 3 hours or until thickened.

In a large bowl, combine the bananas, blueberries, peaches, strawberries, grapes and the pineapple chunks. Spread pudding mixture over the top. Garnish with mint if desired. **Yield: 12-14 servings.**

NUTRITION FACTS: 1 serving equals 149 calories, 3 g fat (2 g saturated fat), 11 mg cholesterol, 107 mg sodium, 30 g carbohydrate, 2 g fiber, 2 g protein.

Pudding-Topped Fruit Salad

Berry Slaw

Caesar Chicken Potato Salad

Sarita Johnston ✳ SAN ANTONIO, TEXAS

Lettuce, chicken and creamy Caesar dressing give a twist to this quick-to-fix potato salad. It's a favorite any time of year.

4	cups quartered small white *or* red potatoes
3/4	pound boneless skinless chicken breasts, cubed
1	tablespoon vegetable oil
1	package (10 ounces) mixed salad greens
1	small red onion, sliced and separated into rings
3/4	cup Caesar salad dressing
1/3	cup croutons
2	tablespoons shredded Parmesan cheese

Place potatoes in a large saucepan and cover with water. Bring to a boil. Reduce heat; cover and cook for 15-20 minutes or until tender. Drain.

Meanwhile, in a skillet, saute chicken in oil for 5-10 minutes or until juices run clear. Add potatoes to chicken.

Place greens and onion in a serving bowl. Top with chicken mixture. Drizzle with dressing; toss to coat. Sprinkle with croutons and Parmesan cheese. **Yield: 4 servings.**

Berry Slaw

Harriet Stichter ✳ MILFORD, INDIANA

As a family, we try to cut down on the fat in our diets without giving up good taste. This refreshing cabbage salad, featuring strawberries and cranberries, is a great warm-weather pick-me-up.

USES LESS FAT, SUGAR OR SALT. INCLUDES NUTRITION FACTS.

1/4	cup cider vinegar
1/4	cup unsweetened apple *or* cranberry juice
1	teaspoon sugar
1/2	teaspoon salt
1/4	teaspoon white pepper
6	cups shredded cabbage
1-1/2	cups sliced fresh strawberries
1/2	cup dried cranberries

In a large bowl, combine the vinegar, apple juice, sugar, salt and pepper; add cabbage. Toss gently to coat. Cover and refrigerate for at least 8 hours or overnight, stirring occasionally. Before serving, stir in strawberries and cranberries. **Yield: 6 servings.**

NUTRITION FACTS: 3/4 cup equals 74 calories, trace fat (trace saturated fat), 0 cholesterol, 212 mg sodium, 17 g carbohydrate, 4 g fiber, 2 g protein.

fresh IDEA

Strawberries stay fresher longer if they are stored unwashed, with the stems on, in a sealed glass jar in the refrigerator. To quickly hull strawberries, insert a straw into the tip of the berry and push it through the other end.

Caesar Chicken Potato Salad

Three-Pepper Pasta Salad

Jan Malone ✳ ARAPAHO, OKLAHOMA

I like to make this recipe during the summer when I can get the ingredients fresh from the garden. The pasta salad not only tastes very good, but it has a pretty presentation, too.

1	package (12 ounces) tricolor spiral pasta
1/3	cup olive oil
3	tablespoons red wine vinegar
1/4	cup minced fresh basil *or* 1 tablespoon dried basil
2	tablespoons grated Parmesan cheese
1-1/4	teaspoons salt
1/4	teaspoon pepper
1	small sweet red pepper, julienned
1	small sweet yellow pepper, julienned
1	small green pepper, julienned
1	medium tomato, cut into thin wedges
1	can (2-1/4 ounces) sliced ripe olives, drained
2	tablespoons sliced green onions
8	ounces cubed part-skim mozzarella cheese

Cook pasta according to package directions. Meanwhile, in a blender, add the oil, vinegar, basil, Parmesan cheese, salt and pepper; cover and process until blended. Drain and rinse pasta in cold water; place in a large bowl. Add the peppers, tomato, olives and onions. Drizzle with dressing; toss to coat. Stir in mozzarella cheese. Serve at room temperature. **Yield: 6-8 servings.**

Lime Delight

Lime Delight

Nancy Vavrinek ✳ ADRIAN, MICHIGAN

Created by my husband's cousin, this refreshing favorite appeared in her church's cookbook. Since it's quick and easy to prepare, I make it often for my husband and me now that we are "empty nesters." It's light and delicious.

1	can (8 ounces) crushed pineapple, undrained
1/4	cup lime gelatin powder
1/2	cup cream-style cottage cheese
1	cup whipped topping

In a small saucepan, bring pineapple to a boil over medium heat. Remove from the heat; stir in gelatin until dissolved. Chill until slightly thickened, about 30 minutes. Stir in cottage cheese and whipped topping. Cover and refrigerate until thickened. **Yield: 2 servings.**

Hash Brown Potato Salad

Joan Hallford ✳ NORTH RICHLAND HILLS, TEXAS

I've used this recipe for more than 20 years, and it's still a family mainstay. It stirs up and cooks in the microwave in a jiffy—and tastes just as good as a traditional German potato salad.

5	bacon strips, diced
6	green onions, sliced
1	package (1 pound) frozen cubed hash brown potatoes, thawed

Three-Pepper Pasta Salad

1/4   cup white wine vinegar

1/2   teaspoon celery salt

Place bacon in a 1-1/2-qt. microwave-safe bowl. Cover and microwave on high for 3-4 minutes or until bacon is crisp. Remove with a slotted spoon to paper towels to drain. Add onions to the drippings; cover and microwave on high for 30 seconds.

Add the potatoes; cover and cook on high for 6-7 minutes, stirring several times. Add the white wine vinegar, celery salt and diced bacon; toss to coat. **Yield: 4 servings.**

EDITOR'S NOTE: This recipe was tested in a 1,100-watt microwave.

Melon Salad with Ginger Dressing

Elsie Mauriello ✳ ATKINSON, NEW HAMPSHIRE

With a hint of honey, this cool, creamy dressing complements the colorful melon and tender chicken. Family and friends will be happy to see it on your table again and again.

DRESSING:

2/3   cup mayonnaise

2/3   cup sour cream

Juice of 1 lime

2   teaspoons honey

1/2   teaspoon ground ginger

1/2   teaspoon salt

1/4   teaspoon pepper

SALAD:

3   boneless skinless chicken breast halves

1   cup apple juice

1   cup water

1   teaspoon whole black peppercorns

2   celery ribs, sliced

2   cups cantaloupe balls

2   cups honeydew balls

1/4   cup chopped fresh parsley

Lettuce leaves, optional

In a small bowl, combine all dressing ingredients; cover and chill. In a large covered saucepan, simmer chicken in apple juice, water and peppercorns for 20 minutes or until chicken juices run clear.

Discard broth; allow chicken to cool. Slice into thin strips and place in a large bowl. Add celery, melon balls and parsley. Serve on a bed of lettuce if desired. Drizzle with dressing. **Yield: 6-8 servings.**

Irish Potato Salad

Irish Potato Salad

Nancy Martin ✳ MARTELLE, IOWA

By combining potatoes, corned beef and cabbage, this hearty salad is a perfect dish for St. Patrick's Day. Everyone in my family favors the one-of-a-kind flavor.

3   large potatoes

2   tablespoons white vinegar

2   teaspoons sugar

1   teaspoon mustard seed

1/2   teaspoon celery seed

3/4   teaspoon salt, *divided*

3   cups cubed cooked corned beef

3   cups chopped cabbage

1/2   cup chopped radishes, optional

3/4   cup mayonnaise

1/3   cup dill pickle relish

1/4   cup sliced green onions

4   teaspoons milk

3/4   teaspoon Dijon mustard, optional

Place potatoes in a large saucepan and cover with water. Bring to a boil. Reduce heat; cover and cook for 15-20 minutes or until tender. Drain; cool slightly. Peel and cube potatoes. Transfer to a large bowl. In a small bowl, combine the vinegar, sugar, mustard seed, celery seed and 1/2 teaspoon salt; pour over warm potatoes and toss to coat. Cover and chill.

Just before serving, stir in the corned beef, cabbage and radishes if desired. In a small bowl, combine the mayonnaise, relish, onions, milk, mustard if desired and remaining salt; pour over salad and toss to coat. **Yield: 8 servings.**

Cucumber Potato Salad

Cucumber Potato Salad

Martha Campbell ✳ BELTON, SOUTH CAROLINA

When my husband had heart surgery, I had to look for recipes that were nutritious yet tasty. With just a touch of mayonnaise, this one filled the bill. When I use the microwave to cook the potatoes, I can serve it up in no time.

2	medium red potatoes, cooked and cubed
2	to 3 tablespoons mayonnaise
1	tablespoon dill pickle relish
1	tablespoon diced pimientos
1/2	teaspoon celery seed
1/2	teaspoon dill weed
1/4	teaspoon salt
1	medium cucumber, sliced
2	tablespoons chopped pecans, toasted

In a large bowl, combine the first seven ingredients. Place cucumber slices in a fan shape on two salad plates; top with potato salad. Sprinkle with pecans. **Yield: 2 servings.**

Chicken Tortellini Salad

Mary Bilke ✳ EAGLE RIVER, WISCONSIN

This is one of the many dishes we offer at the salad bar in the restaurant where I work. It seems to disappear before our eyes!

8	ounces tortellini, cooked, drained and cooled
1	cup cubed cooked chicken

3/4	cup frozen peas, thawed
1/2	cup mayonnaise
1/2	cup diced part-skim mozzarella cheese
1/2	cup Parmesan ranch salad dressing
2	tablespoons minced green onions
2	tablespoons finely chopped sweet red pepper
1	tablespoon minced fresh parsley

Combine all ingredients in a large bowl. Refrigerate until ready to serve. **Yield: 6 servings.**

Apple Coleslaw

Ann Main ✳ MOOREFIELD, ONTARIO

Chopped apple, celery and green pepper add extra crunch to this crisp coleslaw. The lemony, home-made dressing has plenty of celery seed and a hint of honey.

2	cups coleslaw mix
1	unpeeled tart apple, chopped
1/2	cup chopped celery
1/2	cup chopped green pepper
1/4	cup vegetable oil
2	tablespoons lemon juice
2	tablespoons honey
1	teaspoon celery seed

In a large bowl, combine the coleslaw mix, apple, celery and green pepper. In a small bowl, whisk remaining ingredients. Pour over coleslaw; toss to coat. **Yield: 4-6 servings.**

Apple Coleslaw

Ambrosia Compote

Ambrosia Compote

Marilou Robinson ✳ PORTLAND, OREGON

This delightful medley of pineapple, oranges, bananas and grapes gets a refreshing spark from ginger ale, while flaked coconut adds tropical flair. Whether it's served at a brunch or potluck, this salad is always well received.

1	can (20 ounces) pineapple chunks
3	medium firm bananas, sliced
1	cup seedless red grapes
3	medium navel oranges, peeled and sectioned
1	cup flaked coconut, *divided*
1/2	cup ginger ale, chilled
1	tablespoon sliced star fruit, optional

Drain pineapple; reserving juice. In a large bowl, add the bananas, pineapple, grapes, oranges and half the coconut; pour reserved juice over the fruit; lightly toss to coat. Cover and refrigerate for up to 4 hours.

Just before serving, pour ginger ale over salad and sprinkle with remaining coconut. Serve with a slotted spoon. Garnish with star fruit if desired. **Yield: 6-8 servings.**

salad STAR

When selecting star fruit, the more golden-colored the fruit is, the sweeter it will be. There's no need to peel the shiny skin, but you may want to remove the brown fibers from the ridges before slicing.

Ham 'n' Hominy Salad

Anita Freed ✳ KALAMAZOO, MICHIGAN

I love collecting recipes, and this is one I found several years ago. This fresh-tasting mix is one of my favorites.

USES LESS FAT, SUGAR OR SALT. INCLUDES NUTRITION FACTS.

1	medium onion, chopped
1	tablespoon butter
1	tablespoon all-purpose flour
1/2	cup water
1/4	cup cider vinegar
1/4	cup sugar
1/4	teaspoon salt
1/8	teaspoon pepper
1	can (15-1/2 ounces) hominy, rinsed and drained
1	cup cubed fully cooked ham
1/2	cup chopped celery
1/2	cup chopped green pepper

In a large skillet, saute onion in butter until tender. Stir in flour until blended. In a small bowl, combine the water, vinegar and sugar. Whisk into the onion mixture. Bring to a boil; cook and stir for 2 minutes or until thickened. Remove from the heat; stir in the remaining ingredients. Serve warm or cold. **Yield: 4-6 servings.**

NUTRITION FACTS: 1 cup equals 142 calories, 4 g fat (2 g saturated fat), 17 mg cholesterol, 736 mg sodium, 21 g carbohydrate, 3 g fiber, 6 g protein.

Ham 'n' Hominy Salad

Picnic Pasta Salad

Luana Francis ✳ COLUMBIA STATION, OHIO

I like recipes that use what we grow. This particular recipe has been handed down in our family for years. I can't go to a picnic without it.

- 3 cups tricolor spiral pasta, cooked and drained
- 1 package (10 ounces) frozen corn, thawed
- 2 cups cherry tomatoes, halved
- 2 small zucchini, sliced
- 1 cup small pitted ripe olives

DRESSING:
- 1/3 cup tarragon vinegar
- 1/2 cup olive oil
- 2 teaspoons dill weed
- 1 teaspoon salt
- 1/2 teaspoon sugar
- 1/2 teaspoon ground mustard
- 1/4 teaspoon pepper
- 1/4 teaspoon garlic powder

In a large bowl, toss pasta, corn, tomatoes, zucchini and olives; set aside. In a jar with a tight-fitting lid, combine all of the dressing ingredients; cover and shake well. Drizzle over salad; lightly toss to coat. Cover and refrigerate at least 2 hours or overnight. **Yield: 6-8 servings.**

Sweet Potato Slaw

Sweet Potato Slaw

Brenda Sharon ✳ CHANNING, MICHIGAN

I grew up in Louisiana, and we ate lots of sweet potatoes. Prepared in this distinctive salad, they look like carrots.

- 1/2 cup mayonnaise
- 1/2 cup sour cream
- 2 tablespoons honey
- 2 tablespoons lemon juice
- 1 teaspoon grated lemon peel
- 1/2 teaspoon salt
- 1/4 teaspoon pepper
- 3 cups shredded peeled uncooked sweet potatoes
- 1 medium apple, peeled and chopped
- 3/4 cup pineapple tidbits, drained
- 1/2 cup chopped pecans

In a large bowl, whisk the first seven ingredients until smooth. In a large bowl, combine the potatoes, apple, pineapple and pecans. Add dressing; toss to coat. Cover and refrigerate for at least 1 hour. **Yield: 6-8 servings.**

Creamy Waldorf Salad

Linda Stateler ✳ OTTUMWA, IOWA

Things do not get much easier than preparing this pleasantly dressed fruit salad. Crunchy red apples and walnuts contrast nicely with juicy grapes and chewy raisins.

USES LESS FAT, SUGAR OR SALT. INCLUDES NUTRITION FACTS.

- 1 large red apple, chopped
- 1/2 cup halved seedless red grapes
- 1/2 cup whipped topping
- 1/4 cup raisins
- 1/4 cup mayonnaise
- 3 tablespoons coarsely chopped walnuts

Picnic Pasta Salad

In a large bowl, combine all the ingredients. Chill until serving. **Yield: 3 servings.**

NUTRITION FACTS: 3/4 cup (prepared with reduced-fat whipped topping and fat-free mayonnaise) equals 177 calories, 7 g fat (2 g saturated fat), 0 cholesterol, 142 mg sodium, 31 g carbohydrate, 3 g fiber, 2 g protein.

Oriental Pasta Salad

Diane Molberg ✳ CALGARY, ALBERTA

With a wonderful combination of flavors and even colors, this pasta side dish goes great with barbecued chicken or pork.

USES LESS FAT, SUGAR OR SALT. INCLUDES NUTRITION FACTS.

2	cups uncooked elbow macaroni
2	large carrots, cut into 1-inch strips
1	cup snow peas, halved
2	green onions with tops, sliced
1/2	cup thinly sliced sweet red pepper

DRESSING:

1/2	cup mayonnaise
1/2	cup sour cream
1	tablespoon cider vinegar
1	tablespoon soy sauce
1/2	teaspoon ground ginger
1/4	teaspoon pepper

Cook macaroni according to package directions; drain and rinse in cold water. Place in a large bowl; add carrots, peas, onions and red pepper. In a small bowl, whisk dressing ingredients until smooth. Pour over salad and toss to coat. Cover and refrigerate for 1-2 hours. **Yield: 7 servings.**

NUTRITION FACTS: 1 cup (prepared with fat-free mayonnaise, nonfat sour cream and light soy sauce) equals 139 calories, 1 g fat, 1 mg cholesterol, 216 mg sodium, 27 g carbohydrate, 5 g protein.

Oriental Pasta Salad

Strawberry-Rhubarb Gelatin

Strawberry-Rhubarb Gelatin

Kathy Flowers ✳ BURKESVILLE, KENTUCKY

The rosy color and tangy flavor of this favorite comes through with every refreshing bite. It's a quick and simple addition to any meal. Our family and friends look forward to this dish when joining us for dinner on the farm.

USES LESS FAT, SUGAR OR SALT. INCLUDES NUTRITION FACTS.

1	cup chopped fresh *or* frozen rhubarb
3/4	cup water
1	package (3 ounces) strawberry gelatin
1/3	cup sugar
1	tablespoon strawberry jam *or* strawberry spreadable fruit
1	cup unsweetened pineapple juice
1	medium tart apple, diced
1/2	cup chopped walnuts, optional

Lettuce leaves and mayonnaise, optional

In a saucepan over medium heat, bring rhubarb and water to a boil. Reduce heat; cover and simmer for 8-10 minutes or until rhubarb is tender. Remove from the heat. Add the gelatin powder, sugar and jam; stir until gelatin is dissolved. Add pineapple juice. Chill until partially set.

Stir in apple and nuts if desired. Pour into six 1/2-cup molds or a 1-qt. bowl coated with nonstick cooking spray. Chill until set. Unmold onto lettuce leaves if desired and top with a dollop of mayonnaise. **Yield: 6 servings.**

NUTRITION FACTS: 1 serving (prepared with sugar-free strawberry gelatin and spreadable strawberry fruit, and without nuts and mayonnaise) equals 96 calories, trace fat (0 saturated fat), 0 cholesterol, 33 mg sodium, 24 g carbohydrate, 1 g protein.

EDITOR'S NOTE: If using frozen rhubarb, measure rhubarb while still frozen, then thaw completely. Drain in a colander, but do not press the liquid out.

Basil Pasta and Ham Salad

Basil Pasta and Ham Salad

Pauline Piggott ✳ NORTHVILLE, MICHIGAN

With fresh basil and tomatoes in the dressing, this refreshing pasta dish delightfully captures the flavor of summer.

USES LESS FAT, SUGAR OR SALT. INCLUDES NUTRITION FACTS.

TOMATO BASIL DRESSING:
1	cup chopped fresh tomatoes
1/4	cup chopped fresh basil
2	tablespoons chopped green onions
2	tablespoons olive oil
2	tablespoons lemon juice
1	garlic clove, minced
1/2	teaspoon sugar
1/4	teaspoon salt, optional
1/4	teaspoon pepper

SALAD:
2-1/2	cups uncooked spiral pasta
1	cup cubed fully cooked ham
1	can (2-1/4 ounces) sliced ripe olives, drained
1/3	cup chopped fresh basil

In a large bowl, combine tomatoes, basil, onions, oil, lemon juice, garlic, sugar, salt and pepper if desired. Cover and refrigerate for at least 15 minutes. Meanwhile, cook pasta according to package directions until firm to the bite; drain and rinse with cold water. Transfer to a large salad bowl. Stir in the ham, olives and basil. Pour dressing over salad; toss to coat. **Yield: 8 servings.**

NUTRITION FACTS: 1/8 recipe (calculated w/o added salt) equals 186 calories, 6 g fat (0 saturated fat), 8 mg cholesterol, 333 mg sodium, 26 g carbohydrate, 8 g protein.

Apple-Strawberry Peanut Salad

Mardi DesJardins ✳ WINNIPEG, MANITOBA

This recipe originally called just for apples, but I added the strawberries for extra color and flavor. Folks say the salty nuts create a delicious contrast with the sweet fruit, and I have to say that I couldn't agree more.

3	medium apples, cubed
1	to 2 cups sliced strawberries
1	cup thinly sliced celery
1/2	cup mayonnaise
3	tablespoons honey
3/4	teaspoon celery seed
3/4	cup salted peanuts

In a large bowl, combine apples, strawberries and celery. In a small bowl, combine mayonnaise, honey and celery seed; mix well.

Just before serving, add peanuts to fruit mixture and drizzle with dressing. **Yield: 6-8 servings.**

Citrus Chiffon Salad

Kathy Newman ✳ CEDARBURG, WISCONSIN

Crushed pineapple, orange juice and a hint of lemon, give this creamy gelatin salad a pleasant tang. The cool, fluffy side dish is sure to win raves with friends at your next get-together or even from your family over a simple weeknight dinner.

1	cup orange juice
1	tablespoon lemon juice
1	package (.3 ounce) sugar-free lemon *or* orange gelatin
1	package (8 ounces) fat-free cream cheese, cubed
1	cup reduced-fat whipped topping
1	can (8 ounces) unsweetened crushed pineapple, undrained
1/3	cup reduced-fat mayonnaise

In a small saucepan, bring orange and lemon juices to a boil; stir in gelatin until dissolved.

In a blender, process the cream cheese, whipped topping, pineapple and mayonnaise until smooth.

Add gelatin mixture; cover blender and process mixture until blended.

Pour into a 4-cup mold coated with nonstick cooking spray. Refrigerate for several hours or overnight until firm. **Yield: 8 servings.**

Avocado Fruit Salad

Mediterranean Medley Salad

Merwyn Garbini ✳ TUCSON, ARIZONA

This winning alternative to pasta salad is perfect for casual summer luncheons. You can serve it as a main dish with the tuna or without it for a hearty side. Sometimes, I substitute reduced-fat mayonnaise for the olive oil.

USES LESS FAT, SUGAR OR SALT. INCLUDES NUTRITION FACTS.

2	cups cooked brown rice
1	can (6 ounces) light water-packed tuna, drained and flaked
1/2	cup sliced ripe olives
1/2	cup sliced celery
1/2	cup frozen peas, thawed
1	medium tomato, diced
1/2	cup chopped green pepper
1/4	cup thinly sliced radishes
1/4	cup sliced green onions
1/4	cup grated carrots

LEMON HERB SALAD DRESSING:

2	tablespoons olive oil
2	tablespoons water
2	tablespoons lemon juice
1	tablespoon Italian seasoning
1	teaspoon sugar
1/2	teaspoon salt
1	garlic clove, minced
1/4	teaspoon lemon-pepper seasoning

In a large bowl, combine the first 10 ingredients. In a jar with a tight-fitting lid, combine salad dressing ingredients; shake well. Pour over salad and toss to coat. Cover and refrigerate for at least 1 hour. **Yield: 4 servings.**

NUTRITION FACTS: 1-1/2 cups equals 284 calories, 11 g fat (2 g saturated fat), 18 mg cholesterol, 669 mg sodium, 33 g carbohydrate, 5 g fiber, 14 g protein.

Avocado Fruit Salad

Mildred Sherrer ✳ ROANOKE, TEXAS

Avocado may seem like an unusual addition to a fruit salad, but it makes this recipe absolutely outstanding! The lemony dressing really jazzes up the combination.

3	medium ripe avocados, pitted and peeled
2	tablespoons lemon juice
1/2	cup plain yogurt
2	tablespoons honey
1	teaspoon grated lemon peel
1	medium apple, chopped
1	medium firm banana, cut into 1/4-inch slices
1	cup halved seedless grapes
1	can (11 ounces) mandarin oranges, drained

Cut avocados into chunks. Place in a large bowl; drizzle with lemon juice and toss to coat. Drain, reserving the lemon juice; set avocados aside.

For dressing, in a small bowl, combine the yogurt, honey, lemon peel and reserved lemon juice. In another large bowl, toss the apple, banana, grapes, oranges and avocados. Serve with dressing. **Yield: 6 servings.**

avocado ADVICE

The easiest avocados to peel and slice are those that are ripe yet firm. Remove the peel by scooping out the flesh from each half with a large metal spoon, staying close to the peel. Dip slices in lemon juice to keep them from turning brown.

Mediterranean Medley Salad

6 breakfast on the go

Feeling rushed? Busy mornings are no excuse for not eating breakfast...especially when you can take one of these warm, handheld breakfast sandwiches with you. Fluffy eggs, savory sausage, crisp bacon—even waffles and pancakes—create some eye-opening daybreak sensations.

page 75

page 79

page 80

Brunch Pizza Squares

Brunch Pizza Squares

LaChelle Olivet ✴ PACE, FLORIDA

This is one morning mainstay everyone will wake up for! Convenient crescent rolls make a delicious crust for the cheese and sausage topping on this open-faced-sandwich specialty.

- 1 pound bulk pork sausage
- 1 tube (8 ounces) refrigerated crescent rolls
- 4 eggs
- 2 tablespoons milk
- 1/8 teaspoon pepper
- 3/4 cup shredded cheddar cheese

In a large skillet, crumble sausage and cook over medium heat until no longer pink; drain. Unroll crescent dough onto the bottom and 1/2 in. up the sides of a lightly greased 13-in. x 9-in. x 2-in. baking pan; seal seams. Sprinkle with sausage.

In a large bowl, beat the eggs, milk and pepper; pour over sausage. Sprinkle with cheese.

Bake, uncovered, at 400° for 15 minutes or until a knife inserted in the center comes out clean. **Yield: 8 servings.**

Apple Sausage Pitas

Michelle Komaroski ✴ PUEBLO, COLORADO

This is such a simple recipe, but it's my favorite breakfast for family or company. Filled with sausage and apple slices, the handheld bites are great to munch on the way to work or school.

- 1 package (8 ounces) brown-and-serve sausage links, sliced
- 4 medium tart apples, peeled and thinly sliced

- 1/4 cup maple syrup
- 6 pita breads (6 inches), halved

In a large skillet, cook sausage and apples over medium heat until sausage is heated through and apples are tender. Add syrup; heat though. In a microwave, warm pitas on high for 15-20 seconds. Fill with the sausage mixture. **Yield: 4 servings.**

Waffle Sandwiches

Robyn Parish ✴ DALY CITY, CALIFORNIA

Start your day off right by combining three classic breakfast foods into one—eggs, bacon and waffles. I think the sandwiches are delicious served with maple syrup.

- 1 tablespoon butter
- 8 eggs
- 1/4 teaspoon salt

Dash pepper

- 8 frozen waffles
- 8 bacon strips, cooked and drained

Maple syrup

In a large nonstick skillet, melt butter over medium-high heat. Whisk the eggs, salt and pepper. Add egg mixture to skillet (mixture should set immediately at edges).

As eggs set, push cooked edges toward the center, letting uncooked portion flow underneath. When the eggs are set, cut into four wedges.

Meanwhile, prepare waffles according to package directions. For each sandwich, place one waffle on a plate. Layer with an omelet wedge, two bacon strips and a waffle. Serve with syrup. **Yield: 4 servings.**

Waffle Sandwiches

Zesty Breakfast Burritos

Zesty Breakfast Burritos

Angie Ibarra ✳ STILLWATER, MINNESOTA

My husband grew up in Mexico and prefers his food extra spicy. Special seasonings easily added to ordinary ground pork give some zip to standard sausage and eggs.

2	tablespoons vinegar
1	tablespoon chili powder
1	teaspoon dried oregano
1	teaspoon salt
1	garlic clove, minced
1	pound ground pork
6	eggs
1/4	cup milk
1	tablespoon vegetable oil
6	flour tortillas (8 inches), warmed

Taco sauce

In a large bowl, combine the vinegar, chili powder, oregano, salt and garlic; crumble pork over mixture and mix well. Cover and chill overnight.

In a large skillet, cook pork mixture over medium heat until meat is no longer pink. Drain; set aside and keep warm. In a large bowl, whisk eggs and milk. In a another large skillet, heat oil until hot.

Add egg mixture; cook and stir over medium heat until eggs are completely set.

Spoon about 1/4 cup pork mixture and 1/4 cup egg mixture down the center of each tortilla. Top with taco sauce and roll up. **Yield: 6 servings.**

Omelet Biscuit Cups

Leila Zimmer ✳ YORK, SOUTH CAROLINA

My husband's a busy farmer and sometimes eats his breakfast on the run. He's able to take these omelet biscuit cups with him in his truck or in his tractor cab.

1	tube (12 ounces) large refrigerated buttermilk biscuits
4	eggs
1/4	cup milk
1/8	teaspoon salt
1/8	teaspoon pepper
1	cup diced fully cooked ham
3/4	cup shredded cheddar cheese, *divided*
1/3	cup chopped canned mushrooms
1	tablespoon butter

Press biscuits onto the bottom and up the sides of greased muffin cups; set aside. In a large bowl, beat the eggs, milk, salt and pepper. Add ham, 1/4 cup cheese and mushrooms; mix well. In a skillet, melt butter; add the egg mixture. Cook and stir until eggs are nearly set. Spoon into biscuit cups.

Bake at 375° for 10-15 minutes or until biscuits are golden brown. Sprinkle with remaining cheese. Bake 2 minutes longer or until cheese is melted. **Yield: 5 servings.**

Omelet Biscuit Cups

smart START

Leftover dinner biscuits make great grab-and-go breakfast items. Simply warm them in the microwave or toaster. Top them with a little butter or your favorite jam, and you have a no-fuss, economical meal on-the-run.

Breakfast Loaf

Amy McCuan ✳ OAKLEY, CALIFORNIA

I love to make this hearty loaf when we have company for the weekend. I serve it with juice and fresh fruit. At about a dollar per serving, it's priced right. If you like, add sliced mushrooms, olives or chopped onion.

6	eggs, lightly beaten
1/4	teaspoon salt
1/8	teaspoon pepper
1	tablespoon butter
1	round loaf (1 pound) French bread
6	ounces thinly sliced deli ham, *divided*
3/4	cup shredded Monterey Jack cheese, *divided*
3/4	cup shredded cheddar cheese, *divided*
1/2	medium sweet red pepper, thinly sliced
1	medium tomato, thinly sliced

In a small bowl, combine eggs, salt and pepper. Melt butter in a skillet; add eggs. Cook and stir until set; set aside. Cut the top fourth off loaf of bread. Carefully hollow out top and bottom, leaving a 1/2-in. shell. (Discard removed bread or save for another use.) Set top aside.

In bottom of bread, place a fourth of the ham. Layer with half of the Monterey Jack and cheddar cheese, red pepper, scrambled eggs and tomato slices. Top with the remaining cheese and ham. Gently press the layers together. Replace bread top and wrap tightly in foil. Bake at 350° for 25-30 minutes or until heated through. Let stand for 10 minutes before cutting. **Yield: 6 servings.**

Breakfast Loaf

French Toast Sandwiches

French Toast Sandwiches

Deborah Fagan ✳ LANCASTER, PENNSYLVANIA

Thick slices of French toast make a deliciously different breakfast sandwich. Featuring Canadian bacon and Monterey Jack cheese, the sandwiches are paired with strawberry preserves for a sweet-and-salty combo that can't be beat!

12	slices Canadian bacon
6	slices Monterey Jack cheese
12	slices French bread (1/2 inch thick)
3/4	cup eggnog
3	tablespoons butter
6	tablespoons strawberry preserves

Place two slices of Canadian bacon and one slice of cheese on each of six slices of bread. Top with remaining bread. Place eggnog in a shallow dish. Dip sandwiches in eggnog.

In a large skillet or griddle, melt 2-3 tablespoons butter. Toast sandwiches until bread is lightly browned on both sides, adding butter if necessary. Serve with strawberry preserves. **Yield: 6 servings.**

EDITOR'S NOTE: This recipe was tested with 3/4 cup commercially prepared eggnog.

Breakfast in a Biscuit

Janeil Rasmussen ✳ POCATELLO, IDAHO

This recipe brings back memories of my youth. My mother used to make these muffins as a special breakfast treat, but my husband and I also have them for dinner.

2	cups all-purpose flour
1	tablespoon baking powder
1	teaspoon salt

1/4   cup shortening

3/4   cup milk

3/4   pound bulk pork sausage, cooked and drained

1/2   cup shredded Colby-Monterey Jack cheese

2   tablespoons sliced green onion

2   eggs, lightly beaten

Melted butter

In a large bowl, combine the flour, baking powder and salt. Cut in shortening until mixture resembles coarse crumbs. Stir in milk to form a soft dough. Divide into 12 portions.

Roll each into a 6-in. circle; press onto the bottoms and up the sides of greased muffin cups. Fill each with 2 tablespoons sausage and about 1 teaspoon cheese. Sprinkle with onion. Spoon about 2 teaspoons beaten egg over each.

Pinch crust together over filling to seal; brush with butter. Bake at 400° for 18-22 minutes before removing from pan to a wire rack. Serve warm. Refrigerate leftovers. **Yield: 1 dozen.**

Omelet Quesadilla

In a small bowl, beat egg white and water; lightly brush over edges of dough. Top with scrambled eggs and two sausage links. Fold dough over; seal edges and press together with a fork.

Place on an ungreased baking sheet. Brush with remaining egg white mixture. Bake at 375° for 14-16 minutes or until golden brown. **Yield: 8 servings.**

Smoked Sausage Pockets

Jan Badovinac ✳ HARRISON, ARKANSAS

These sausage-and-egg pockets are always a hit. The golden crust has a complete meal hidden inside, so it's perfect for folks on the run.

2   packages (3 ounces *each*) cream cheese, softened

1-1/2   teaspoons minced fresh parsley

3/4   teaspoon seasoned salt

1/4   teaspoon pepper

2/3   cup shredded cheddar cheese

2   tablespoons butter

5   eggs, beaten

1   tube (17.3 ounces) large refrigerated biscuits

1   egg white

1   teaspoon water

16   miniature smoked sausage links

In a large mixing bowl, beat the cream cheese, parsley, seasoned salt and pepper until blended. Stir in cheddar cheese; set aside. In a large skillet, heat butter until hot. Add eggs; cook and stir over medium heat until eggs are completely set.

Separate biscuits into eight pieces. On a lightly floured surface, roll each piece into a 5-in. circle. On each circle, spread about 2 tablespoons of cream cheese mixture to within 1/2 in. of edges.

Omelet Quesadilla

Terri Capps ✳ WICHITA, KANSAS

I came up with these crispy quesadillas because my family found breakfast burritos too messy. They're fast to fix, fun to eat, filling and healthy... and you can add or subtract ingredients to fit individual tastes.

1   cup sliced fresh mushrooms

2   tablespoons chopped onion

1/2   cup egg substitute

2   tablespoons chopped fresh tomato

2   flour tortillas (10 inches)

4   thin slices lean ham (1/2 ounce *each*)

1/4   cup shredded part-skim mozzarella cheese

1/4   cup shredded reduced-fat cheddar cheese

3   tablespoons salsa

In a small nonstick skillet coated with cooking spray, cook mushrooms and onion over medium heat until tender. Add egg substitute and tomato; cook and stir until eggs are set.

Place one tortilla in a large ungreased nonstick skillet; top with ham, egg mixture, cheeses and remaining tortilla. Cook over medium heat, carefully turning once, until lightly browned on both sides and cheese is melted. Cut into four wedges. Serve with salsa. **Yield: 2 servings.**

Bacon Avocado Burritos

Bacon Avocado Burritos

Cleo Gossett ✳ EPHRATA, WASHINGTON

These savory breakfast bundles are quick to make and fun to take when you're on the go. The tortillas are dipped in beaten eggs, then cooked to give them color and flavor. I set out a variety of filling ingredients and toppings and let everyone assemble their own.

4	eggs
8	flour tortillas (7 inches)
1	to 2 tablespoons vegetable oil
1-1/2	cups (6 ounces) shredded cheddar cheese
1	large ripe avocado, thinly sliced
1-1/2	cups chopped green onions
1	package (1 pound) sliced bacon, cooked and crumbled

Salsa, ranch salad dressing *or* sour cream

In a shallow bowl, beat eggs. Dip one tortilla in eggs. In a large skillet, cook tortilla in oil on both sides just until egg sets. Remove and place between paper towels to drain; keep warm. Repeat with remaining tortillas, adding more oil if needed.

Place the cheese, avocado, onions and bacon down the center of tortillas; top with salsa, salad dressing or sour cream. Fold ends and sides over filling and roll up. Filled burritos may be warmed in the microwave just before serving if desired. **Yield: 8 servings.**

Ham Wafflewiches

Janell Willford ✳ PIEDMONT, MISSOURI

Now that I'm retired, it seems I'm busier than ever. But I always make the time to cook for my family. My kids and grandchildren think these "wafflewiches" are a fun treat.

1-1/2	cups finely chopped fully cooked ham
1	can (4 ounces) mushroom stems and pieces, drained and finely chopped
1/3	cup mayonnaise
1/4	cup chopped celery
1	tablespoon chopped onion
16	frozen waffles
2	tablespoons butter
2	tablespoons all-purpose flour
1/4	teaspoon salt
1-1/2	cups milk
4	teaspoons prepared mustard, optional
1/2	cup shredded cheddar cheese, optional

In a large bowl, combine the ham, mushrooms, mayonnaise, celery and onion. Spread mixture on eight waffles; top with remaining waffles. Place on a greased baking sheet. Bake at 400° for 15-20 minutes or until browned.

Meanwhile, melt butter in a saucepan over medium heat. Stir in flour and salt until smooth. Gradually add milk. Bring to a boil; boil and stir for 2 minutes. Remove from the heat. Add mustard and cheese if desired; stir until smooth. Serve with wafflewiches. **Yield: 8 servings.**

EDITOR'S NOTE: Reduced-fat or fat-free mayonnaise is not recommended for this recipe.

Ham Wafflewiches

Baked Brunch Sandwiches

Baked Brunch Sandwiches

Carolyn Herfkens ✳ CRYSLER, ONTARIO

Serving brunch to your bunch is a breeze when you prepare this recipe the night before. They combine the flavor of grilled ham and cheese with the puffy texture of French toast.

3	tablespoons Dijon mustard
12	slices bread
6	slices fully cooked ham
12	slices cheddar *or* Swiss cheese
1	medium tomato, thinly sliced
3	tablespoons butter, softened
4	eggs
1/4	cup milk
1/4	teaspoon pepper

Spread mustard on one side of six slices of bread. Layer the ham, cheese and tomato over mustard; top with remaining bread. Butter the outsides of the sandwiches; cut in half. Arrange in a greased 13-in. x 9-in. x 2-in. baking dish.

In a small bowl, whisk the eggs, milk and pepper; pour over sandwiches. Cover and refrigerate overnight.

Remove from the refrigerator 30 minutes before baking. Bake, uncovered, at 375° for 30 minutes or until a knife inserted in the center comes out clean. **Yield: 6 servings.**

Huevos Rancheros

Liane Davenport ✳ GREENSBORO, NORTH CAROLINA

This quesadilla-like breakfast dish is packed with tongue-tingling Southwest flavor. I like to serve it with sour cream and extra picante sauce or salsa.

1	tablespoon butter
4	eggs, lightly beaten
1	cup (4 ounces) shredded cheddar cheese
1	small tomato, seeded and chopped (about 1/2 cup)
1/4	cup picante sauce
2	flour tortillas (8 inches)
3	tablespoons sour cream

Additional picante sauce

In a large skillet, heat butter until hot. Add eggs; cook and stir over medium heat until eggs are completely set. In a large bowl, combine the scrambled eggs, cheese, tomato and picante sauce.

Spray one side of a tortilla with nonstick cooking spray. Place tortilla greased side down on a griddle. Spoon half the egg mixture on half of the tortilla.

Fold over and cook over low heat for 1-2 minutes on each side or until cheese is melted and tortilla is golden brown. Repeat with remaining tortilla and egg mixture. Cut into wedges and serve with sour cream and additional picante sauce. **Yield: 2 servings.**

sunny SALAD

For a breakfast you can assemble at home and enjoy at work, simply mix some fresh berries or fruit with yogurt in a small food storage container the night before. As you leave the house, top it all off with a handful of granola.

Huevos Rancheros

Confetti Scrambled Egg Pockets

Dixie Terry ✳ GOREVILLE, ILLINOIS

This sunny specialty is a colorful crowd-pleaser. My eight grandchildren often enjoy these egg-packed pitas for Saturday morning brunch...or with a light salad for supper.

USES LESS FAT, SUGAR OR SALT. INCLUDES NUTRITION FACTS.

1	cup fresh *or* frozen corn
1/4	cup chopped green pepper
2	tablespoons chopped onion
1	jar (2 ounces) diced pimientos, drained
1	tablespoon butter
1-1/4	cups egg substitute
3	eggs
1/4	cup fat-free evaporated milk
1/2	teaspoon seasoned salt
1	medium tomato, seeded and chopped
1	green onion, sliced
3	whole wheat pita breads (6 inches), halved

In a large nonstick skillet, saute the corn, green pepper, onion and pimientos in butter for 5-7 minutes or until tender.

In a large bowl, combine the egg substitute, eggs, milk and salt; pour into skillet. Cook and stir over medium heat until eggs are completely set. Stir in the tomato and green onion. Spoon about 2/3 cup into each pita half. **Yield: 6 servings.**

NUTRITION FACTS: 1 filled pita half equals 207 calories, 6 g fat (2 g saturated fat), 112 mg cholesterol, 538 mg sodium, 28 g carbohydrate, 4 g fiber, 13 g protein.

Confetti Scrambled Egg Pockets

Sausage Egg Subs

Dee Pasternak ✳ BRISTOL, INDIANA

Spicy chunks of sausage give winning flavor to this scrambled egg mixture. Served in a hoagie bun, it's a satisfying, all-in-one sandwich for breakfast or even lunch.

1-1/4	pounds bulk pork sausage
1/4	cup chopped onion
12	eggs, lightly beaten
1/2	cup chopped fresh mushrooms
1	to 2 tablespoons finely chopped green pepper
1	to 2 tablespoons finely chopped sweet red pepper
6	submarine sandwich buns (about 6 inches), split

In a large skillet, cook sausage and onion over medium heat until the meat is no longer pink; drain. Remove with a slotted spoon and keep warm.

In the same skillet, cook and stir the eggs over medium heat for 6-7 minutes or until nearly set. Add mushrooms, peppers and the sausage mixture. Cook until eggs are completely set and mixture is heated through. Serve on buns. **Yield: 6 servings.**

Banana Raisin Wraps

Peggy Burdick ✳ BURLINGTON, MICHIGAN

For a quick pick-me-up, try these roll-ups. The peanut butter and banana combination is a fun change from the savory fillings you usually find in tortillas.

1/2	cup peanut butter
4	flour tortillas (8 inches)
2	medium firm bananas, cut into 1/4-inch slices
1/4	cup raisins

Spread peanut butter over one side of each tortilla. Arrange banana slices and raisins over peanut butter, pressing lightly. Roll up loosely; cut in half. **Yield: 4 servings.**

Scrambled Egg Brunch Bread

Julie Deal ✳ CHINA GROVE, NORTH CAROLINA

This attractive braid is brimming with eggs, ham and cheese, making it a real meal in one. By using refrigerated crescent rolls, it's a snap to prepare.

- 2 tubes (8 ounces *each*) refrigerated crescent rolls
- 4 ounces thinly sliced deli ham, julienned
- 4 ounces cream cheese, softened
- 1/2 cup milk
- 8 eggs
- 1/4 teaspoon salt

Dash pepper

- 1/4 cup chopped sweet red pepper
- 2 tablespoons chopped green onion
- 1 teaspoon butter
- 1/2 cup shredded cheddar cheese

Unroll each tube of crescent dough (do not separate rectangles). Place side by side on a greased baking sheet with long sides touching; seal seams and perforations. Arrange ham lengthwise down center third of rectangle.

In a large mixing bowl, beat cream cheese and milk until smooth. Separate one egg; set egg white aside. Beat the egg yolk, remaining eggs, salt and

Spinach Egg Croissants

pepper into cream cheese mixture. Stir in red pepper and onions.

In a large skillet, melt butter; add egg mixture. Cook and stir over medium heat just until set. Remove from the heat. Spoon scrambled eggs over ham. Sprinkle with cheese.

On each long side of dough, cut 1-in.-wide strips to the center to within 1/2 in. of filling. Starting at one end, fold alternating strips at an angle across the filling. Pinch ends to seal and tuck under.

Beat reserved egg white; brush over dough. Bake at 375° for 25-28 minutes or until golden brown. **Yield: 6 servings.**

Spinach Egg Croissants

Karen Oviatt ✳ WASHOUGAL, WASHINGTON

This special breakfast entree is a real treat on weekends when I have time to enjoy a relaxing meal.

- 1 cup sliced fresh mushrooms
- 1 package (10 ounces) fresh spinach, chopped
- 1 small onion, chopped
- 2 to 3 tablespoons vegetable oil
- 10 eggs, beaten
- 1 cup (4 ounces) shredded Monterey Jack cheese
- 8 croissants, split
- 2 cups prepared hollandaise sauce

In a large skillet, saute mushrooms, spinach and onion in oil until tender. Add eggs; cook and stir over medium heat until eggs are completely set. Stir in cheese.

Toast croissant halves under broiler until golden brown. Top with egg mixture and hollandaise sauce. **Yield: 8 servings.**

Scrambled Egg Brunch Bread

7 wraps, pitas & specialty sandwiches

When the usual sandwich just won't do, turn to these swift wraps, stuffed pitas, piled-high bagels and other fresh ideas.

page 90

page 93

page 84

Chicken Cheddar Wraps

Chicken Cheddar Wraps

Ruth Andrewson ✳ LEAVENWORTH, WASHINGTON

I keep cooked chicken in the freezer, so these mildly spiced sandwiches are simple to assemble in the summer when you have to get a meal on the table in a hurry. Children love them and often eat more than one.

USES LESS FAT, SUGAR OR SALT. INCLUDES NUTRITION FACTS.

1	cup (8 ounces) sour cream
1	cup chunky salsa
2	tablespoons mayonnaise
4	cups cubed cooked chicken
2	cups (8 ounces) shredded cheddar cheese
1	cup thinly sliced fresh mushrooms
2	cups shredded lettuce
1	cup guacamole, optional
12	flour tortillas (6 inches), room temperature

Tomato wedges and additional guacamole, optional

In a large bowl, combine the sour cream, salsa and mayonnaise. Stir in chicken, cheese and mushrooms. Divide the lettuce and the guacamole if desired between tortillas. Place about 1/2 cup chicken mixture on each tortilla.

Fold sides over the filling. Garnish with tomato wedges and additional guacamole if desired. **Yield: 12 wraps.**

NUTRITION FACTS: 1 wrap (prepared with fat-free sour cream and reduced-fat mayonnaise and cheese and without guacamole and tomato) equals 271 calories, 6 g fat (0 saturated fat), 34 mg cholesterol, 537 mg sodium, 35 g carbohydrate, 2 g fiber, 18 g protein.

Citrus Fish Tacos

Maria Baldwin ✳ MESA, ARIZONA

Fun fish tacos bring change-of-pace flair to everyone's favorite Southwest standby! I combine the halibut or cod with a zesty seasoning and add a fruity salsa that is tucked inside the wholesome corn tortillas.

1-1/2	cups finely chopped fresh pineapple
1	can (11 ounces) mandarin oranges, drained and cut in half
1	envelope reduced-sodium taco seasoning, *divided*
3	tablespoons orange juice concentrate, *divided*
3	tablespoons lime juice, *divided*
1	jalapeno pepper, seeded and finely chopped
1-1/2	pounds halibut *or* cod, cut into 3/4-inch cubes
8	corn tortillas (6 inches), warmed
3	cups shredded lettuce

In a large bowl, combine the pineapple, oranges, 1 tablespoon taco seasoning, 1 tablespoon orange juice concentrate, 1 tablespoon lime juice and jalapeno pepper. Cover and refrigerate.

Place fish in an ungreased shallow 2-qt. baking dish. In a small bowl, combine the remaining orange juice concentrate, lime juice and taco seasoning. Pour over fish; toss gently to coat. Cover and bake at 375° for 12-16 minutes or until fish flakes easily with a fork.

Place a spoonful of fish mixture down the center of each tortilla. Top with lettuce and pineapple salsa; roll up. **Yield: 4 servings.**

EDITOR'S NOTE: When cutting or seeding hot peppers, use rubber or plastic gloves to protect your hands. Avoid touching your face.

Citrus Fish Tacos

Cran-Orange Turkey Bagel

Cran-Orange Turkey Bagel

Tanya Smeins ✳ WASHINGTON, NORTH CAROLINA

I adapted the recipe for this tasty turkey sandwich from a deli where I worked. To make it easier to eat, we often dip each bite into the cranberry mixture instead of spreading it inside.

- 1   can (11 ounces) mandarin oranges, drained
- 1   can (16 ounces) whole-berry cranberry sauce
- 6   tablespoons cream cheese, softened
- 6   onion bagels *or* flavor of your choice, split and toasted
- 1   pound thinly sliced cooked turkey

In a bowl, mash mandarin oranges with a fork. Stir in cranberry sauce. Spread cream cheese over the bottom of each bagel; top with turkey and cran-orange sauce. Replace bagel tops. **Yield: 6 servings.**

Ham Pecan Pitas

Bea John ✳ DIXON, ILLINOIS

For a delightfully different twist on ham salad, try this hearty variation featuring crunchy pecans, hard-cooked egg and cheddar cheese.

- 1   cup diced fully cooked ham
- 1   hard-cooked egg, chopped

- 1/2   cup shredded sharp cheddar cheese
- 1/2   cup chopped pecans
- 2/3   cup sour cream
- 2   tablespoons chopped green onions
- 4   pita breads, halved

In a large bowl, combine the first six ingredients. Spoon into pita bread. **Yield: 4 servings.**

Pork Pocket Pasties

Dolores Haynie ✳ BANNING, CALIFORNIA

During my life I have spent many joyful hours in the kitchen. I most often cook from scratch, but I can't resist these delectable pasties that call for frozen hash browns.

- 1   pound bulk pork sausage
- 2   cups frozen hash browns, thawed
- 1   large carrot, finely chopped
- 1/4   cup chopped onion
- 1/2   teaspoon salt
- 1/4   teaspoon pepper
- 1-1/2   cups (6 ounces) shredded Monterey Jack cheese
- 4   pita breads (6 inches), halved
- 1   tablespoon butter

Crumble sausage into a large skillet; cook over medium heat until no longer pink; drain. Add the hash browns, carrot, onion, salt and pepper. Cook until vegetables are tender, stirring occasionally. Remove from the heat; stir in cheese. Spoon into pitas.

Place on an ungreased baking sheet; brush outside of pitas with butter. Bake at 400° for 4-5 minutes or until heated through. **Yield: 8 servings.**

Pork Pocket Pasties

tortilla TIP

If your flour tortillas are too stiff to roll into wraps, place them between two damp microwave-safe paper towels and warm them in the microwave oven. Check them every few seconds and remove them when they are pliable.

Raisin Bagel Stackers

Cynthia DeKett ✳ LYNDONVILLE, VERMONT

This stacked sandwich began by accident when I ran out of bread and replaced it with a bagel. You can easily change the fixings to meet your personal tastes. My husband prefers it with less meat, a slice of Vidalia onion and no cream cheese. We both think the raisin bagel adds the perfect touch of sweetness.

2	cinnamon raisin bagels (3-1/2 inches), split
4	teaspoons reduced-fat cream cheese
4	lettuce leaves
1/4	pound shaved deli smoked turkey
2	fresh dill sprigs
2	green onions, sliced
2	slices (1/2 ounce *each*) reduced-fat Swiss cheese
4	thin tomato slices
1/8	teaspoon salt
1/8	teaspoon pepper
2	teaspoons reduced-fat mayonnaise

Lightly toast bagels; spread cream cheese on bottom halves. Layer with the lettuce, turkey, dill, onions, cheese and tomato. Sprinkle with salt and pepper. Spread mayonnaise on top halves of bagels; place over tomato. **Yield: 2 servings.**

Fry Bread Sandwiches

Fry Bread Sandwiches

Sandra Cameron ✳ FLAGSTAFF, ARIZONA

It was traditional for Native American girls in our village to learn to cook at an early age. I made fry bread many times for my father and seven brothers, and after I perfected the recipe, Father said it was the best he'd ever eaten.

3	cups all-purpose flour
1	teaspoon baking powder
1/2	teaspoon salt
1-1/4	cups milk

Oil for deep-fat frying

12	lettuce leaves
12	slices deli turkey *or* ham
6	slices cheddar cheese
1	small onion, sliced and separated into rings
18	thin slices tomato
1	can (4 ounces) chopped green chilies

In a large bowl, combine the flour, baking powder and salt. Add milk and stir to form a soft dough. Cover and let rest for 1 hour.

Divide dough into six portions. On a lightly floured surface, roll each portion into an 8-in. circle.

In an electric skillet or deep-fat fryer, heat oil to 375°. Fry bread circles, one at a time, until golden, turning once; drain on paper towels. Keep warm.

Cut each circle in half. On six halves, layer the lettuce, turkey, cheese, onion and tomato; sprinkle with chilies. Top with remaining bread. **Yield: 6 servings.**

Raisin Bagel Stackers

Chicken Apricot Bundles

Brenda Lawson ✳ JEFFERSON CITY, MISSOURI

My husband enjoys these warm sandwiches for his lunch. These handheld favorites are so easy to prepare, I don't mind making them often.

- 2   tubes (8 ounces *each*) refrigerated crescent rolls
- 1   can (10 ounces) chunk white chicken, drained and chopped
- 1/2   cup shredded cheddar cheese
- 1   package (3 ounces) cream cheese, softened
- 1/4   cup chopped dried apricots
- 1/4   cup chopped pecans
- 1/4   teaspoon celery seed

Unroll crescent roll dough and separate into eight rectangles. Place on an ungreased baking sheet; sealing perforations.

In a small bowl, combine the remaining ingredients; spoon 1/4 cupful onto the center of each rectangle. Bring edges to the center; pinch to seal. Bake at 375° for 12-15 minutes or until golden. **Yield: 8 servings.**

Pork Salad Rolls

Katie Koziolek ✳ HARTLAND, MINNESOTA

Our sons request these sandwiches so much I often prepare extra pork roast with this recipe in mind. They especially like the recipe when the pork salad is wrapped in tortillas.

- 1/2   cup mayonnaise
- 1   teaspoon Dijon mustard
- 1/2   teaspoon lemon juice
- 1/2   teaspoon seasoned salt
- 1/4   teaspoon pepper
- 3   cups shredded cooked pork
- 1/2   cup thinly sliced celery
- 1/2   cup halved seedless green grapes
- 6   flour tortillas (6 inches) *or* hard rolls, split

Lettuce leaves, optional

In a large bowl, combine the mayonnaise, mustard, lemon juice, seasoned salt and pepper. Add the pork, celery and grapes; toss to coat. Refrigerate for at least 1 hour.

Spoon 1/2 cup pork mixture down the center of each tortilla; add lettuce if desired; roll up. **Yield: 6 servings.**

Meat Loaf Gyros

Meat Loaf Gyros

Willa Fershee ✳ CORUNNA, INDIANA

Being one-time caterers, my husband and I were asked to supervise our church's youth group suppers. This is the recipe I prepared for Greek Night. It was a hit with everyone.

- 1/4   cup water
- 1/4   cup finely chopped onion
- 2   tablespoons minced fresh parsley
- 2   teaspoons salt
- 1   teaspoon ground cumin
- 1   teaspoon dried oregano
- 3/4   teaspoon pepper
- 1/4   teaspoon garlic powder
- 2   pounds lean ground beef
- 1   large red onion, chopped
- 1   large tomato, thinly sliced
- 8   pita breads, halved
- 1/2   cup plain yogurt

In a large bowl, combine the first eight ingredients. Crumble beef over mixture and mix well.

Press into an ungreased 9-in. x 5-in. x 3-in. loaf pan. Bake at 350° for 1-1/4 to 1-1/2 hours or until meat is no longer pink; drain.

Let stand for 10 minutes. Cut into thin slices. Place meat loaf, onion and tomato into pita halves; drizzle with yogurt. **Yield: 8 servings.**

EDITOR'S NOTE: Creamy cucumber or ranch salad dressing can be used in place of the yogurt.

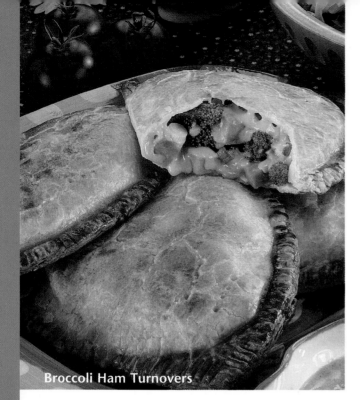
Broccoli Ham Turnovers

Caesar Chicken Wraps

Christi Martin ✳ ELKO, NEVADA

When we have chicken for dinner, I cook extra for these full-flavored roll-ups. Featuring Caesar salad dressing, cream cheese, red pepper, black olives and a hint of garlic, the wraps are perfect alongside corn on the cob and a green vegetable.

1/2	cup Caesar salad dressing
1/2	cup grated Parmesan cheese, *divided*
1	teaspoon lemon juice
1	garlic clove, minced
1/4	teaspoon pepper
1	package (8 ounces) cream cheese, softened
3	cups shredded romaine
1/2	cup diced sweet red pepper
1	can (2-1/4 ounces) sliced ripe olives, drained
5	flour tortillas (10 inches)
1-3/4	cups cubed cooked chicken

In a small bowl, combine the salad dressing, 1/4 cup Parmesan cheese, lemon juice, garlic and pepper. In a small mixing bowl, beat cream cheese until smooth. Add half of the salad dressing mixture and mix well; set aside.

In a large bowl, combine the romaine, red pepper and olives. Add the remaining salad dressing mixture; toss to coat. Spread about 1/4 cup cream cheese mixture on each tortilla. Top with the romaine mixture and chicken; sprinkle with remaining Parmesan cheese. Roll up; cut in half. **Yield: 5 servings.**

Broccoli Ham Turnovers

Lupie Molinar ✳ TUCSON, ARIZONA

I enjoy creating special dishes for my family and friends. Although I don't make sandwiches often, these attractive turnovers with their fresh-tasting filling are an exception everyone seems to enjoy.

2	cups broccoli florets
1-1/2	cups (6 ounces) shredded sharp cheddar cheese
1/2	cup cubed fully cooked ham
1/2	cup sliced green onions
1	tablespoon minced fresh parsley
1/4	teaspoon ground nutmeg

Salt and pepper to taste

Pastry for double-crust pie

1	egg
1	tablespoon heavy whipping cream

Place broccoli in a steamer basket over 1 in. of boiling water in a saucepan. Cover and steam for 5-8 minutes or until crisp-tender. Rinse in cold water; drain well. In a bowl, combine broccoli, cheese, ham, onions, parsley, nutmeg, salt and pepper.

On a floured surface, roll out pastry; cut each in half. Place 1-1/2 cups filling on one side of each half; flatten filling with a spoon. Combine egg and cream; brush some over pastry edges. Fold pastry over filling. Seal edges and prick tops with a fork.

Place on a baking sheet; brush with remaining egg mixture. Bake at 400° for 18-22 minutes or until golden brown. Let stand 5 minutes before serving. **Yield: 4 servings.**

Caesar Chicken Wraps

Italian Chicken Pockets

Italian Chicken Pockets

Tricia Buss ✳ TELFORD, PENNSYLVANIA

My sister-in-law prepared these hearty sandwiches that are filled with chicken, mushrooms and pepperoni. My husband loved them so much, he insisted I ask for the recipe.

3/4	pound boneless skinless chicken breast, cubed
2	tablespoons olive oil
1	medium green pepper, chopped
1	cup sliced fresh mushrooms
1	package (3-1/2 ounces) sliced pepperoni
1	cup spaghetti sauce
3	pita breads (6 inches), halved and warmed

Grated Parmesan cheese, optional

In a large skillet, cook chicken over medium heat in oil until chicken juices run clear. Add green pepper and mushrooms; cook until tender; stirring occasionally. Stir in pepperoni; cook until heated through. Drain. Stir in spaghetti sauce; cook until heated through.

Spoon into the pita bread halves. Sprinkle with Parmesan cheese if desired. **Yield: 6 servings.**

wrap PARTY

For a new take on your favorite wrap, leave the tortillas behind and grab a slice of bread. Remove the bread's crust, and roll the bread flat. Add your sandwich fixings, roll it all up and secure with a toothpick or even a pretzel stick.

Hacienda Hot Dogs

Kelly Williams ✳ LA PORTE, INDIANA

This yummy creation with taco sauce and refried beans makes inexpensive hot dogs taste great. I sometimes like to wrap the hot dogs with a strip of bacon before baking them.

8	Chicago-style beef hot dogs (4 ounces *each*)
1	cup (4 ounces) shredded Colby-Monterey Jack cheese
1	bottle (8 ounces) taco sauce
8	hot dog buns, split
1	cup refried beans

Shredded lettuce

1	large tomato, chopped
24	pickled pepper rings

Minced fresh cilantro

Cut a lengthwise slit three-quarters of the way through each hot dog and to within 1/2 in. of each end. Fill pocket with 2 tablespoons cheese.

Place in an ungreased 13-in. x 9-in. x 2-in. baking dish. Pour taco sauce over hot dogs. Bake, uncovered, at 350° for 15-17 minutes or until cheese is melted.

Spread the inside of each bun with 2 tablespoons refried beans. Layer with lettuce, hot dog, tomato, pepper rings and cilantro. **Yield: 8 servings.**

Hacienda Hot Dogs

Bagel Melts

Linda Mincy ✳ COUNCE, TENNESSEE

I use whole wheat bagels or English muffins for these open-faced sandwiches. The quick combo is great for breakfast or alongside soup for dinner.

4	tablespoons prepared mustard
2	bagels, split
8	slices cheddar cheese
8	slices Canadian bacon
8	slices tomato

Spread 1 tablespoon mustard over each bagel half. Layer with one cheese slice, two Canadian bacon slices, two tomato slices and a second cheese slice. Place on an ungreased baking sheet. Bake at 350° for 4-6 minutes or until cheese is melted. **Yield: 4 servings.**

Beef 'n' Cheese Wraps

Sue Sibson ✳ HOWARD, SOUTH CAROLINA

For a lunch you can put together in moments, try these hearty wraps stuffed with roast beef, cheddar cheese and a flavorful cream cheese spread.

4	flour tortillas (10 inches), warmed
1	carton (8 ounces) spreadable chive and onion cream cheese

Beef 'n' Cheese Wraps

Club Quesadillas

1	cup shredded carrots
1	cup (4 ounces) shredded Monterey Jack cheese
1	pound thinly sliced cooked roast beef

Leaf lettuce

Spread one side of each tortilla with cream cheese; layer with the carrots, Monterey Jack cheese, beef and lettuce. Roll up tightly and wrap in plastic wrap. Refrigerate for at least 30 minutes. Cut in half or into 1-inch slices. **Yield: 4 servings.**

Club Quesadillas

Victoria Hahn ✳ NORTHAMPTON, PENNSYLVANIA

Here's a fun spin on the classic club sandwich— turn it into a tasty quesadilla! This speedy recipe featuring all your favorite club fixings is wonderful during warm weather or when you are short on kitchen time.

1/2	cup mayonnaise
8	flour tortillas (8 inches)
4	lettuce leaves
2	medium tomatoes, sliced
8	slices deli turkey
8	slices deli ham
8	slices provolone cheese
8	bacon strips, cooked

Salsa

Spread mayonnaise on each tortilla. Layer lettuce, tomatoes, turkey, ham, cheese and bacon over the mayonnaise; top with remaining tortillas. Cut into quarters. Serve with salsa. **Yield: 4 servings.**

Egg Salad Pitas

Ricquel Stinson ✳ MT. ORAB, OHIO

I came up with this recipe purely by accident. I was making egg salad and just kept adding different seasonings. When my friend tried it, she raved about it.

2/3	cup mayonnaise
2	tablespoons sweet pickle relish
1	teaspoon prepared mustard
1/4	teaspoon pepper
1/4	teaspoon celery salt
1/4	teaspoon paprika
1/4	teaspoon dried basil
1/4	teaspoon salt
6	hard-cooked eggs, coarsely chopped
1/2	cup shredded cheddar cheese
1	small onion, finely chopped
1	large carrot, grated
2	bacon strips, cooked and crumbled
3	pita breads (6 inches), halved

Lettuce leaves and sliced tomatoes, optional

In a bowl, combine the first eight ingredients. Stir in the eggs, cheese, onion, carrot and bacon. Spoon about 1/2 cup into each pita half. Add lettuce and tomatoes if desired. **Yield: 3-6 servings.**

Mother's Pasties

Egg Salad Pitas

Mother's Pasties

Vivienne Abraham ✳ DETROIT, MICHIGAN

Pasties were a must years ago when men worked the mines in northern Michigan. The housewives made them in the morning and wrapped them tightly in newspaper so they would stay warm until lunch break.

3	cups cubed peeled potatoes
1	cup chopped carrots
1	medium onion, chopped
3/4	teaspoon salt
1/4	teaspoon pepper
1/2	pound ground beef
1/4	pound ground pork
1	tablespoon butter, melted

PASTRY:

4	cups all-purpose flour
1-1/4	teaspoons salt
1	cup shortening
3/4	cup cold water

In a large bowl, combine the potatoes, carrots, onion, salt and pepper. Crumble beef and pork over potato mixture and mix well. Add butter and toss to coat; set aside. For pastry, in a large bowl, combine flour and salt. Cut in shortening until mixture resembles coarse crumbs. Gradually add water, tossing with a fork until a ball forms.

Divide dough into five portions; roll each into a 10-in. circle. Place 1 cup of filling in the center of each circle. Fold pastry over filling and seal edges tightly with a fork; cut slits in the top of each.

Place the pasties on a greased baking sheet. Bake at 375° for 50-60 minutes or until golden brown. **Yield: 5 servings.**

Sausage Pepper Calzones

Sausage Pepper Calzones

Marion Lowery ✳ MEDFORD, OREGON

Made from convenient frozen bread dough, these tasty Italian sandwiches are chock-full of savory turkey sausage, sweet peppers and herbs, enhanced by zesty pizza sauce.

1	pound Italian turkey sausage links
1	cup chopped onion
3/4	cup *each* chopped green, sweet red and yellow peppers
2	garlic cloves, minced
5	teaspoons olive oil, *divided*
2	tablespoons sherry *or* chicken broth
1	teaspoon balsamic vinegar
1	teaspoon salt
1/2	teaspoon pepper
3	teaspoons minced fresh oregano, *divided*
3	teaspoons minced fresh rosemary, *divided*
2	loaves (1 pound *each*) frozen bread dough, thawed
1	can (15 ounces) pizza sauce, *divided*
3	teaspoons cornmeal

Remove and discard sausage casings; crumble the sausage. In a large nonstick skillet, cook sausage, onion, peppers and garlic in 2 teaspoons oil over medium heat until meat is no longer pink; drain. Stir in the sherry or broth, vinegar, salt, pepper and 1 teaspoon each of the oregano and rosemary; heat mixture through.

Divide each loaf of dough into six portions. On a floured surface, roll each portion into a 6-in. circle. Brush with remaining oil; sprinkle with remaining oregano and rosemary. Spread 1 tablespoon pizza sauce over each circle. Spoon about 1/4 cup pepper filling on half of each circle to within 1/2 in. of edges; fold dough over filling and seal edges. Cut a small slit in top.

Coat baking sheets with nonstick cooking spray and sprinkle with cornmeal. Place the calzones on baking sheets. Cover and let rise in a warm place for 30 minutes.

Bake at 400° for 12-15 minutes or until golden brown. Warm remaining pizza sauce; serve with calzones. **Yield: 12 servings.**

Olive Chicken Roll-Ups

Lisa Hymson ✳ AURORA, COLORADO

I like to serve these handheld sandwiches with salsa on the side for dipping. Or you can slice them into pinwheels for appetizers.

1	package (8 ounces) cream cheese, softened
2	cans (4 ounces *each*) chopped green chilies, drained
1	can (2-1/4 ounces) chopped ripe olives, drained
1	jar (2 ounces) diced pimientos, drained
1/4	teaspoon garlic powder
1/4	teaspoon chili powder
1/4	teaspoon hot pepper sauce
8	flour tortillas (8 inches)
1-1/4	pounds deli smoked chicken

Salsa *or* picante sauce, optional

In a large mixing bowl, beat cream cheese until smooth. Fold in chilies, olives, pimientos, garlic powder, chili powder and hot pepper sauce.

Spread on one side of each tortilla; top with chicken and roll up tightly. Wrap in plastic wrap; refrigerate for at least 1 hour. Serve with salsa if desired. **Yield: 8 servings.**

Olive Chicken Roll-Ups

Ham and Cheese Bagels

Ham and Cheese Bagels

Kristin Dallum ✳ VANCOUVER, WASHINGTON

These bite-size bagel sandwiches are easy to fix for breakfast, lunch, snacks and family get-togethers. Both combinations of toppings are as yummy as they are colorful.

1	package (3 ounces) cream cheese, softened
6	miniature bagels, split
3	ounces thinly sliced fully cooked ham
4	ounces cheddar cheese, thinly sliced
6	thin slices tomato
1	tablespoon chopped red onion
1/4	cup pineapple tidbits
1/4	teaspoon dried parsley flakes

Spread cream cheese over cut sides of bagels. Place on an ungreased baking sheet with cream cheese side up. Cut the ham and cheddar cheese into 2-in. squares; place over cream cheese.

Top half of the bagels with the tomato slices and onion and half with the pineapple and parsley. Bake at 350° for 10 minutes or until cheese is melted. **Yield: 1 dozen.**

lunch box TREAT

Dress up brown bag staples with this fun idea: Slice off the top of a hard roll and hollow out the inside. Line the shell with lettuce leaves and fill with chicken or tuna salad. Return the top of the roll and wrap with plastic wrap.

Fresh Veggie Pockets

Linda Reeves ✳ CLOVERDALE, INDIANA

One summer I worked at a health food store that sold sandwiches. We were close to a college campus, so I made lots of these fresh pitas for the students. Crunchy with crisp vegetables and nutty sunflower kernels, they're a fast-to-fix meal when you're on the go.

1	carton (8 ounces) spreadable cream cheese
1/4	cup sunflower kernels
1	teaspoon seasoned salt *or* salt-free seasoning blend
4	wheat pita breads, halved
1	medium tomato, thinly sliced
1	medium cucumber, thinly sliced
1	cup sliced fresh mushrooms
1	ripe avocado, peeled and sliced

In a bowl, combine the cream cheese, sunflower kernels and seasoned salt; spread about 2 tablespoons on the inside of each pita half. Layer with tomato, cucumber, mushrooms and avocado. **Yield: 4 servings.**

Fresh Veggie Pockets

8 crowd pleasers

When you have a large, hungry group to feed, turn to this satisfying smorgasbord. Giant sub sandwiches...robust potato and pasta salads...vegetable medleys...flavorful garden salads...and fruity gelatin delights will be the main attractions at your next gathering.

page 104

page 104

page 103

Cheesy Ham Braid

Becky Houston ✳ GRAND JUNCTION, TENNESSEE

Our congregation is full of wonderful cooks, so we enjoy many potluck meals throughout the year. I like to bring this chewy and cheesy braid shared by a family friend.

1	package (16 ounces) hot roll mix
1	cup warm water (120° to 130°)
1	egg, lightly beaten
2	tablespoons butter, softened, *divided*
1/2	cup chopped onion
1/2	cup chopped green pepper
2	cups chopped fully cooked ham
1-1/2	cups (6 ounces) shredded cheddar cheese
1	cup (8 ounces) ricotta cheese
1	tablespoon minced fresh parsley
1	egg white
1	tablespoon cold water

In a large bowl, combine the hot roll mix and contents of yeast packet. Stir in the warm water, egg and 1 tablespoon butter. Turn onto a floured surface; knead until smooth and elastic, about 6-8 minutes; set aside.

In a large skillet, saute onion and green pepper in remaining butter until tender. Remove from the heat; stir in ham, cheeses and parsley.

On a greased baking sheet, roll dough into a 15-in. x 10-in. rectangle. Spoon ham mixture lengthwise down the center of dough. On each long side, cut 1-in.-wide strips about 2 in. into the center. Starting at one end, fold alternating strips at an angle across filling. Pinch ends to seal. Cover and let rise in a warm place for 15 minutes or until almost doubled.

In a small bowl, beat egg white and cold water; brush over dough. Bake at 375° for 25-30 minutes or until golden brown. Let stand for 10 minutes before slicing. Serve warm. Refrigerate leftovers. **Yield: 6-8 servings.**

Kiwi-Strawberry Spinach Salad

Laura Pounds ✳ ANDOVER, KANSAS

This pretty salad is always a hit when I serve it! The recipe came from a cookbook, but I "doctored" it up to personalize it. Sometimes just a small change in ingredients can make a big difference.

USES LESS FAT, SUGAR OR SALT. INCLUDES NUTRITION FACTS.

12	cups torn fresh spinach
2	pints fresh strawberries, halved
4	kiwifruit, peeled and cut into 1/4-inch slices
1/3	cup sugar
1/4	cup vegetable oil
1/4	cup raspberry vinegar
1/4	teaspoon paprika
1/4	teaspoon Worcestershire sauce
2	green onions, chopped
2	tablespoons sesame seeds, toasted
1	tablespoon poppy seeds

In a large salad bowl, combine the spinach, strawberries and kiwi. In a blender, combine the sugar, oil, vinegar, paprika and Worcestershire sauce; cover and process for 30 seconds. Add onions, sesame seeds and poppy seeds. Pour over salad; toss to coat. Serve immediately. **Yield: 12 servings.**

NUTRITION FACTS: 1 cup equals 121 calories, 6 g fat (trace saturated fat), 0 cholesterol, 64 mg sodium, 16 g carbohydrate, 4 g fiber, 3 g protein.

Kiwi-Strawberry Spinach Salad

Cool Cucumber Pasta

Cool Cucumber Pasta

Jeanette Fuehring ✳ CONCORDIA, MISSOURI

People say this salad is crispy, sweet and refreshingly different. It's the perfect addition to any potluck or large gathering.

8	ounces uncooked penne pasta
1	tablespoon vegetable oil
2	medium cucumbers, thinly sliced
1	medium onion, thinly sliced
1-1/2	cups sugar
1	cup water
3/4	cup white vinegar
1	tablespoon prepared mustard
1	tablespoon dried parsley flakes
1	teaspoon salt
1	teaspoon pepper
1/2	teaspoon garlic salt

Cook the pasta according to package directions; drain and rinse in cold water. Place pasta in a large bowl; stir in oil, cucumbers and onion.

In a jar with a tight-fitting lid, combine the remaining ingredients; shake well. Pour over salad; toss to coat. Cover and chill for 3-4 hours, stirring occasionally. Serve with a slotted spoon. Refrigerate leftovers. **Yield: 8-10 servings.**

crisp CUCUMBERS

If you want the cucumbers in your salad to be crunchy, chill them overnight in ice water. You'll be delighted with the results. For extra flair, you can run a fork through the skin down the length of the cucumber before slicing.

Glazed Corned Beef Sandwiches

Rita Reifenstein ✳ EVANS CITY, PENNSYLVANIA

Fans of good food will cheer when you bring out these full-flavored, hearty favorites. Made of tender corned beef and a special sweet and spicy seasoning, they're always well received.

1	corned beef brisket with spice packet (3 to 4 pounds)
12	peppercorns
4	bay leaves
3	garlic cloves, minced
2	cinnamon sticks (3 inches), broken
1	tablespoon crushed red pepper flakes

Sandwich buns
GLAZE:

1/2	cup packed brown sugar
1/2	teaspoon ground cloves
1/2	teaspoon ground ginger
1/2	teaspoon ground mustard
1/4	teaspoon celery salt
1/4	teaspoon caraway seed

Place corned beef with seasoning packet in a Dutch oven; cover with water. Add seasonings and bring to a boil. Reduce heat; cover and simmer for 4 to 4-1/4 hours or until meat is tender. Drain, discarding juices; blot brisket dry.

In a small bowl, combine glaze ingredients. Rub onto top of warm meat. Grill or broil for 5-10 minutes on each side until glazed. Slice meat and serve warm or chilled on buns. **Yield: 12-16 servings.**

Glazed Corned Beef Sandwiches

Mom's Portable Beef

Lorene Sinclair ✳ BELLEVILLE, ONTARIO

This delicious beef makes great sandwiches for a picnic, potluck or even a camping trip. The meat has a tempting, from-scratch flavor that beats deli cold cuts.

USES LESS FAT, SUGAR OR SALT. INCLUDES NUTRITION FACTS.

1	can (14-1/2 ounces) beef broth
1	medium onion, chopped
1	cup cider vinegar
2	tablespoons minced fresh parsley
1	bay leaf
1	tablespoon mixed pickling spices
1/2	teaspoon dried marjoram
1/2	teaspoon dried savory
1/2	teaspoon salt
1/4	teaspoon pepper
1	beef eye round roast (3 pounds)
12	to 14 sandwich rolls, split

Lettuce, tomato and onion, optional

In a Dutch oven, combine first 10 ingredients; add roast. Cover and bake at 325° for 1-1/2 hours or until meat is tender. Remove roast and cool completely.

Meanwhile, skim fat and strain cooking juices. Discard bay leaf. Thinly slice the beef. Serve on rolls with warmed juices and lettuce, tomato and onion if desired. **Yield: 12-14 servings.**

NUTRITION FACTS: 1 sandwich equals 298 calories, 7 g fat (3 g saturated fat), 44 mg cholesterol, 524 mg sodium, 33 g carbohydrate, 2 g fiber, 25 g protein.

Mom's Portable Beef

Giant Focaccia Sandwich

Giant Focaccia Sandwich

Marina Gelling ✳ ROWLETT, TEXAS

A flavorful Italian flat bread made with oats and molasses makes this recipe something special. I tuck ham, cheese and veggies inside, but you can substitute your favorite sandwich fillings.

5-1/2	cups all-purpose flour
1	cup quick-cooking oats
2	packages (1/4 ounce *each*) active dry yeast
2	teaspoons salt
2-1/4	cups water
1/2	cup molasses
1	tablespoon butter
1	egg, lightly beaten
1	tablespoon dried minced onion
1	tablespoon sesame seeds
1	teaspoon garlic salt

SANDWICH FILLING:

6	tablespoons mayonnaise
2	tablespoons prepared mustard
6	to 8 lettuce leaves
12	to 16 thin slices fully cooked ham
6	to 8 thin slices Swiss *or* cheddar cheese
4	slices red onion, separated into rings
1	medium green pepper, sliced
2	medium tomatoes, thinly sliced

In a large mixing bowl, combine the flour, oats, yeast and salt. In a saucepan, heat the water, molasses and butter to 120°-130°. Add to dry ingredients; beat just until moistened. Place in a greased bowl; turn once to grease top. Cover and let rise in a warm place until doubled, about 45 minutes.

Press dough onto a greased 14-in. pizza pan. Cover and let rise until doubled, about 30 minutes.

Brush with egg. Sprinkle with the onion, sesame seeds and garlic salt. Bake at 350° for 30-35 minutes or until golden brown. Remove to a wire rack to cool.

Split the focaccia in half horizontally; spread mayonnaise and mustard on cut sides. On bottom half, layer the lettuce, ham, cheese, onion, green pepper and tomatoes. Replace bread half. Chill until serving. Cut into wedges. **Yield: 12 servings.**

Pork and Corn Barbecue

Juanita Myres ✳ LAKE CHARLES, LOUISIANA

Traditional barbecued pork is livened up with cumin and corn. Alongside a green salad and chips, this is a hot and hearty meal that's sure to please.

1	boneless pork shoulder roast (about 4 pounds), trimmed
1	tablespoon vegetable oil
3	medium onions, chopped
3	garlic cloves, minced
1	teaspoon salt
1	teaspoon ground cumin
1	teaspoon dried oregano
1/3	cup water
1/4	cup cider vinegar
2	cups barbecue sauce
1	can (15-1/4 ounces) whole kernel corn, drained
16	hard rolls, split

In a Dutch oven, brown roast in oil on all sides; remove. Keep warm and set aside. Saute onions and garlic in drippings until onions are tender.

Return roast to Dutch oven. Add salt, cumin, oregano, water and vinegar. Cover and bake at 350° for 2-1/2 to 3 hours or a meat thermometer reaches 170°.

Remove meat and shred with two forks; set aside. Skim off excess fat from pan juices. Stir in the barbecue sauce, corn and reserved pork; heat through. Serve on rolls. **Yield: 16 servings.**

Seven-Layer Gelatin Salad

Melody Mellinger ✳ MYERSTOWN, PENNSYLVANIA

By alternating fruity layers of gelatin in harvest colors with sweetened sour cream, I've created one eye-catching treat.

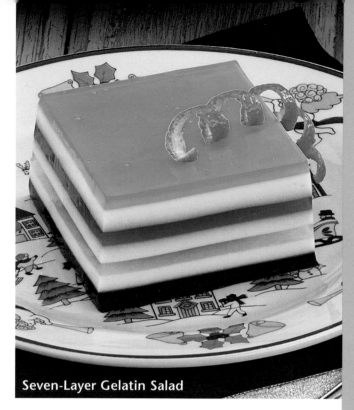

Seven-Layer Gelatin Salad

1	package (3 ounces) cherry gelatin
4	cups boiling water, *divided*
2-1/2	cups cold water, *divided*
2	envelopes unflavored gelatin
2	cups milk
1	cup sugar
2	cups (16 ounces) sour cream
2	teaspoons vanilla extract
1	package (3 ounces) lemon gelatin
1	package (3 ounces) orange gelatin
1	package (3 ounces) lime gelatin

In a bowl, dissolve cherry gelatin in 1 cup boiling water. Add 1/2 cup cold water; stir. Pour gelatin mixture into a 13-in. x 9-in. x 2-in. dish coated with nonstick cooking spray; refrigerate until set but not firm, about 30 minutes.

In a small saucepan, sprinkle unflavored gelatin over 1/2 cup cold water. Let stand for 1 minute. Stir in milk and sugar. Cook and stir over medium heat until gelatin and sugar are dissolved.

Remove from the heat. Whisk in sour cream and vanilla until smooth. Spoon 1-2/3 cups creamy gelatin mixture over the first flavored layer. Chill until set but not firm. Prepare remaining flavored gelatin as directed for cherry gelatin. Alternately layer flavored gelatins with creamy gelatin layers, allowing each to set before adding next layer. Top with lime gelatin. Refrigerate overnight. Cut into squares. **Yield: 12-15 servings.**

EDITOR'S NOTE: This salad takes time to prepare since each layer must be set before the next layer is added. Also remember that the pan will be inverted when unmolded, so put the flavor of gelatin you want on top in the pan first.

Giant Sandwich

Giant Sandwich

Mildred Sherrer ✳ ROANOKE, TEXAS

This lovely layered loaf is definitely not your everyday sandwich. Piled high with a variety of fillings, the wedges are great for a special occasion when served warm from the oven.

1	unsliced round loaf (1-1/2 pounds) rye bread
1	tablespoon prepared horseradish
1/4	pound sliced deli roast beef
2	tablespoons mayonnaise
4	to 6 slices Swiss cheese
2	tablespoons prepared mustard
1/4	pound sliced deli ham
6	bacon strips, cooked
6	slices process American cheese
1	medium tomato, thinly sliced
4	slices red onion, separated into rings
1	tablespoon butter, softened

Cut bread horizontally into six slices. Spread bottom slice with horseradish; top with roast beef. Place the next slice of bread over beef; spread with mayonnaise and top with Swiss cheese. Add next slice of bread; spread with mustard and top with ham. Add the next slice of bread; top with bacon and American cheese. Add next slice of bread; top with tomato and onion.

Spread butter on cut side of bread top; cover sandwich. Place on a baking sheet; loosely tent with heavy-duty foil. Bake sandwich at 400° for 12-14 minutes or until heated through. Carefully slice into wedges. **Yield: 6-8 servings.**

Fruited Pasta Salad

Sandra Pire ✳ BROOKFIELD, WISCONSIN

The vibrant colors, sweet fruit and tender pasta make this festive salad a hit with both men and women at picnics and potlucks.

USES LESS FAT, SUGAR OR SALT. INCLUDES NUTRITION FACTS.

1-1/2	cups uncooked spiral pasta
1	can (8 ounces) unsweetened pineapple chunks
1	carton (8 ounces) fat-free peach yogurt
2	tablespoons fat-free sour cream
1-1/2	cups cubed cantaloupe
1	cup halved seedless grapes
1-1/2	cups sliced fresh strawberries

Cook pasta according to package directions; rinse pasta in cold water and drain. Cool completely. Meanwhile, drain pineapple, reserving 2 tablespoons juice (discard remaining juice or save for another use); set pineapple aside.

In a small bowl, combine the yogurt, sour cream and reserved pineapple juice until smooth; cover and refrigerate.

In a large bowl, combine pasta, pineapple, cantaloupe and grapes. Just before serving, stir in strawberries. Drizzle with yogurt mixture; toss to coat. **Yield: 13 servings.**

NUTRITION FACTS: 1/2 cup serving equals 90 calories, trace fat (0 saturated fat), 1 mg cholesterol, 15 mg sodium, 19 g carbohydrate, 3 g protein.

Fruited Pasta Salad

Golden Apple Potato Salad

Golden Apple Potato Salad

Mary Pipkin ✳ MELBA, IDAHO

This is a wonderful variation on an American summertime standby. Since Idaho is the potato state and a lot of apples are also grown here, I thought this would be an excellent recipe to represent my area.

6	medium potatoes
2/3	cup mayonnaise
1/2	cup plain yogurt
2	tablespoons cider vinegar
2	teaspoons prepared mustard
1	garlic clove, minced
1	teaspoon salt
5	bacon strips, cooked and crumbled
1	medium onion, grated
2	medium golden delicious apples, cubed

Place potatoes in a large saucepan and cover with water. Bring to a boil. Reduce heat; cover and cook potatoes for 15-20 minutes or until tender. Drain. Meanwhile, in a small bowl, combine the mayonnaise, yogurt, vinegar, mustard, garlic and salt.

Peel warm potatoes and slice into a large bowl; add the bacon and onion. Pour dressing over potato mixture; gently toss to coat. Fold in apples. Cover salad and refrigerate for several hours before serving. **Yield: 10 servings.**

potatoes PRONTO

To whip up a batch of potato salad in a jiffy, use canned potatoes instead of spending time peeling and cooking fresh potatoes. They taste the same, and this method keeps the kitchen cool when the weather is warm.

Cranberry Biscuit Turkey Sandwiches

Barbara Nowakowski ✳ NORTH TONAWANDA, NEW YORK

These flavorful buffet bites are so fun and festive! Smoked turkey slices are layered inside biscuits flecked with dried cranberries and spread with a creamy cranberry butter.

USES LESS FAT, SUGAR OR SALT. INCLUDES NUTRITION FACTS.

2	tablespoons cold butter
4	cups biscuit/baking mix
1	cup milk
3/4	cup dried cranberries

CRANBERRY BUTTER:

1/2	cup butter, softened
1/4	cup honey
1/4	cup dried cranberries, chopped
1-1/2	pounds thinly sliced deli smoked turkey

In a large bowl, cut butter into biscuit mix until crumbly; stir in milk just until moistened. Fold in the cranberries. Turn onto a floured surface; knead 10-15 times. Roll out to 1/2-in. thickness; cut with a floured 2-1/2-in. biscuit cutter. Place on ungreased baking sheets. Bake at 400° for 14-16 minutes or until golden brown. Cool on a wire rack.

In a small mixing bowl, beat butter and honey until smooth; stir in cranberries. To assemble sandwiches; split biscuits. Spread with cranberry butter and top with turkey; replace biscuit tops. **Yield: 20 sandwiches.**

NUTRITION FACTS: 1 turkey sandwich equals 223 calories, 10 g fat (5 g saturated fat), 29 mg cholesterol, 621 mg sodium, 24 g carbohydrate, 1 g fiber, 9 g protein.

Cranberry Biscuit Turkey Sandwiches

Frosted Strawberry Salad

Roasted Potato Salad

Terri Adams ✳ SHAWNEE, KANSAS

I pack this delicious potato salad in a cooler to dish up cold at picnics. But because it's so versatile, I sometimes transfer it to a slow cooker to serve it warm at church potlucks.

USES LESS FAT, SUGAR OR SALT. INCLUDES NUTRITION FACTS.

1/2	pound fresh green beans, cut into 1-1/2-inch pieces
1	large whole garlic bulb
2	pounds small red potatoes, quartered
2	medium sweet red peppers, cut into large chunks
2	green onions, sliced
1/4	cup chicken broth
1/4	cup balsamic vinegar
2	tablespoons olive oil
2	teaspoons sugar
1	teaspoon minced fresh rosemary *or* 1/4 teaspoon dried rosemary, crushed
1/2	teaspoon salt

In a large saucepan, bring 6 cups water to a boil. Add beans; bring to a boil. Cover and cook for 3 minutes. Drain and immediately place beans in ice water; drain and pat dry.

Remove papery outer skin from garlic (do not peel or separate cloves). Cut top off garlic bulb. Place cut side up in a greased 15-in. x 10-in. x 1-in. baking pan. Add the potatoes. Bake, uncovered, at 400° for 30 minutes or until garlic is softened.

Remove garlic; set aside. Add red peppers, onions and beans; drizzle with broth. Bake vegetables 30-35 minutes longer or until tender. Cool for

Roasted Potato Salad

10-15 minutes. Squeeze softened garlic into a large bowl. Stir in the vinegar, oil, sugar, rosemary and salt. Add vegetables; toss to coat. Serve warm or cold. **Yield: 9 servings.**

NUTRITION FACTS: 3/4 cup equals 124 calories, 3 g fat (trace saturated fat), 0 cholesterol, 167 mg sodium, 22 g carbohydrate, 3 g fiber, 3 g protein.

Frosted Strawberry Salad

Barbara Towler ✳ DERBY, OHIO

My daughter has requested that her grandmother make this sweet, rich gelatin with its fluffy topping for every family get-together. So at her wedding, this delightful salad was part of the bountiful, potluck buffet.

2	packages (6 ounces *each*) strawberry gelatin
3	cups boiling water
2	packages (10 ounces *each*) frozen sweetened sliced strawberries, thawed
1	can (20 ounces) crushed pineapple, undrained
1	cup chopped pecans
1/2	cup chopped maraschino cherries

TOPPING:

1	package (8 ounces) cream cheese, softened
1	jar (7 ounces) marshmallow creme
1	carton (8 ounces) frozen whipped topping, thawed

Fresh strawberries and mint

In a large bowl, dissolve gelatin in boiling water. Stir in strawberries and pineapple. Refrigerate until partially set.

Stir in pecans and cherries. Transfer to a 13-in. x 9-in. x 2-in. dish. Cover and refrigerate for about 2 hours or until firm.

For topping, in a small mixing bowl, beat cream cheese and marshmallow creme just until combined; fold in whipped topping. Spread over salad.

Cover and refrigerate for several hours or overnight. Cut into squares. Garnish with strawberries and mint. **Yield: 16-20 servings.**

Bean 'n' Corn Salad

Glenda Parsonage ✳ MAPLE CREEK, SASKATCHEWAN

I stir together a colorful medley of beans, peppers, corn and other vegetables, then marinate it overnight in a tasty, sweet dressing. It's a refreshing, change-of-pace side dish.

1	can (16 ounces) kidney beans, rinsed and drained
1	can (14-1/2 ounces) cut green beans, drained
1	can (14-1/2 ounces) wax beans, drained
1	can (11 ounces) whole kernel corn, drained
2	celery ribs, thinly sliced
1	medium green pepper, chopped
1/2	cup chopped sweet red pepper
1/2	cup sliced ripe olives
1/2	cup sliced green onions, optional
1	cup sugar
1	cup white vinegar
2	tablespoons vegetable oil
1/2	teaspoon ground mustard
1/4	teaspoon salt

In a large bowl, combine the first nine ingredients. In a jar with a tight-fitting lid, combine the sugar, vinegar, oil, mustard and salt; cover and shake well until sugar is dissolved. Pour over bean mixture and gently toss to coat. Cover and refrigerate overnight. Serve with a slotted spoon. **Yield: 14 servings.**

Bean 'n' Corn Salad

Stuffed Bread Boat

Stuffed Bread Boat

Elaine Bent ✳ MIDDLEBORO, MASSACHUSETTS

While I was up with one of our babies more than 20 years ago, I heard this "secret" family recipe shared on an all-night talk show. None of our 12 children or our growing troop of grandchildren ever pass up this special stuffed bread.

USES LESS FAT, SUGAR OR SALT. INCLUDES NUTRITION FACTS.

1	loaf (1 pound) unsliced Italian bread
1	pound ground beef
1	large onion, chopped
1	medium green pepper, chopped
1	cup chopped fresh spinach
1	medium tomato, chopped
1/2	teaspoon dried oregano

Salt and pepper to taste

Cut a thin slice off the top of bread; set top aside. Hollow out the loaf, leaving a 1/4-in. shell. Dice removed bread and set aside.

In a nonstick skillet, cook beef over medium heat until no longer pink; drain. Add the onion, green pepper, spinach and tomato; cook 3-4 minutes longer or until vegetables are crisp-tender. Stir in the oregano, salt, pepper, and reserved diced bread.

Spoon beef mixture into bread shell; replace top. Wrap tightly in heavy-duty foil. Bake at 400° for 20 minutes or until heated through. Cut loaf into slices. **Yield: 6-8 servings.**

NUTRITION FACTS: 1 serving equals 258 calories, 7 g fat (3 g saturated fat), 28 mg cholesterol, 374 mg sodium, 32 g carbohydrate, 2 g fiber, 16 g protein.

EDITOR'S NOTE It's easy to mix and match ingredients in the Stuffed Bread Boat. For instance, add some chopped fresh mushrooms or, for lots of color, use a mix of peppers.

Bow Tie Garden Pasta

Bow Tie Garden Pasta

Miriam Hershberger ✳ HOLMESVILLE, OHIO

Just-picked veggies, pleasing bow tie pasta and flavorful seasonings mix together to make a delicious dish. To top it off, it's easy and fun to fix. Our daughter likes to make the pasta on a regular basis.

1	cup Italian salad dressing
2	tablespoons olive oil
1	cup packed fresh basil leaves
2	tablespoons grated Parmesan cheese
2	tablespoons chopped walnuts
1	tablespoon minced garlic
2	cups quartered fresh mushrooms
1	cup fresh broccoli florets
1	cup fresh cauliflowerets
1	medium onion, julienned
1	small green pepper, julienned
1	small zucchini, sliced
1	yellow summer squash, sliced
3	carrots, julienned
1	can (14 ounces) water-packed artichoke hearts, rinsed, drained and quartered
4	cups cooked multicolor cheese-filled tortellini
2	cups cooked bow tie pasta

In a blender, combine the first six ingredients; process on high until smooth. In a large skillet, saute the vegetables in 1/2 cup salad dressing mixture for 3 to 3-1/2 minutes or until crisp-tender. Add pasta. Drizzle with remaining dressing; toss to coat. Serve warm or cold. **Yield: 14 servings.**

Cranberry Cherry Salad

Betsy Bianco ✳ WHEATON, MISSOURI

I like to make this refreshing favorite for summer get-togethers. It's also a great side dish during the Thanksgiving and Christmas seasons. Everybody just loves it.

1	can (14-1/2 ounces) pitted tart red cherries
1	package (3 ounces) cherry gelatin
1	can (8 ounces) jellied cranberry sauce
1	package (3 ounces) lemon gelatin
1	cup boiling water
1	package (3 ounces) cream cheese, softened
1/3	cup mayonnaise
1	can (8 ounces) crushed pineapple, undrained
1/2	cup whipping cream, whipped
1	cup miniature marshmallows

Drain cherries, reserving juice; set cherries aside. Add water to juice to measure 1 cup; transfer to a saucepan. Bring to a boil. Add cherry gelatin; stir until dissolved. Whisk in the cranberry sauce until smooth. Add cherries; pour into an 11-in. x 7-in. x 2-in. dish. Refrigerate until firm.

In a bowl, dissolve lemon gelatin in boiling water. In a small mixing bowl, beat the cream cheese and mayonnaise. Gradually beat in lemon gelatin until smooth. Stir in pineapple. Refrigerate until almost set. Fold in whipped cream and marshmallows. Spoon over cherry layer. Refrigerate until firm. **Yield: 8-10 servings.**

Cranberry Cherry Salad

Boston Subs

Boston Subs

Sue Erdos ✳ MERIDEN, CONNECTICUT

My mother has been making these wonderful subs since she left her hometown of Boston many years ago. They're quick to prepare and travel well if tightly wrapped in plastic wrap. The recipe is great for parties if you use a loaf of French or Italian bread instead of the individual rolls.

1/2	cup mayonnaise
12	submarine sandwich buns, split
1/2	cup Italian salad dressing, *divided*
1/4	pound *each* thinly sliced bologna, deli ham, hard salami, pepperoni and olive loaf
1/4	pound thinly sliced provolone cheese
1	medium onion, diced
1	medium tomato, diced
1/2	cup diced dill pickles
1	cup shredded lettuce
1	teaspoon dried oregano

Spread mayonnaise on inside of buns. Brush with half of the salad dressing. Layer deli meats and cheese on bun bottoms. Top with onion, tomato, pickles and lettuce. Sprinkle sandwiches with oregano and drizzle with remaining dressing. Replace bun tops. **Yield: 12 sandwiches.**

diced ONIONS

Here is a quick and easy way to dice onions. After slicing the onion on your cutting board, run a pizza cutter back and forth over the slices. Store any leftover diced onions in a clean glass jar in your refrigerator.

German Potato Salad

Donna Cline ✳ PENSACOLA, FLORIDA

A dear friend gave me this authentic German recipe. I take the satisfying salad to many gatherings where it always receives rave reviews.

12	medium potatoes
12	bacon strips
1-1/2	cups chopped onion
1/4	cup all-purpose flour
1/4	cup sugar
1	tablespoon salt
1	teaspoon celery seed
1	teaspoon ground mustard

Pinch pepper

1-1/2	cups water
3/4	cup white vinegar

Chopped fresh parsley

Place potatoes in a large saucepan and cover with water. Bring to a boil. Reduce heat; cover and cook for 15-20 minutes or until tender. Drain. Peel and slice into a large bowl; set aside.

In a large skillet, cook bacon until crisp. Using a slotted spoon, remove bacon to paper towels; drain, reserving 2 tablespoons drippings.

Saute onion in drippings until tender. Stir in the next six ingredients. Gradually stir in water and vinegar; bring to a boil, stirring constantly. Cook and stir 2 minutes more or until thickened. Pour over potatoes; toss to coat. Crumble bacon and gently stir into potatoes. Sprinkle top with parsley. **Yield: 12-14 servings.**

German Potato Salad

Egg Salad for a Crowd

Helen Lamison ✳ CARNEGIE, PENNSYLVANIA

Black olives and vegetables add interest and texture to this big-batch egg salad. It's great for sandwiches and also goes a long way served on crackers as an appetizer.

36	hard-cooked eggs, chopped
6	celery ribs, chopped
3	large carrots, finely shredded
3	small green peppers, finely chopped
3	small onions, finely chopped
3	cans (2-1/4 ounces *each*) sliced ripe olives, drained
3	cups mayonnaise
3/4	cup milk
1	tablespoon ground mustard

Salt and pepper to taste

Lettuce leaves, halved cherry tomatoes and sliced hard-cooked egg, optional

100	bread slices (about 6 loaves)

In a large bowl, combine the first six ingredients. Whisk mayonnaise, milk, mustard, salt and pepper until smooth. Stir into egg mixture. Cover and refrigerate for at least 1 hour. Garnish with lettuce, tomatoes and sliced egg if desired.

For sandwiches, spread about 1/3 cupful egg salad on one bread slice; top with another bread slice. **Yield: 50 sandwiches.**

Egg Salad for a Crowd

Super Italian Sub

Super Italian Sub

Patricia Lomp ✳ MIDDLEBORO, MASSACHUSETTS

I like recipes that can be made ahead of time, and this hoagie offers me that convenience. I just wrap it tightly in plastic wrap and keep it in the refrigerator. At mealtime, all that's left to do is slice and enjoy.

1	loaf (1 pound) unsliced Italian bread
1/3	cup olive oil
1/4	cup cider vinegar
8	garlic cloves, minced
1	teaspoon dried oregano
1/4	teaspoon pepper
1/2	pound fully cooked ham, thinly sliced
1/2	pound thinly sliced cooked turkey
1/4	pound thinly sliced hard salami
1/4	pound sliced provolone cheese
1/4	pound sliced part-skim mozzarella cheese
1	medium green pepper, thinly sliced into rings

Cut bread in half lengthwise; hollow out top and bottom, leaving a 1/2-in. shell (discard removed bread or save for another use).

In a small bowl, combine the oil, vinegar, garlic, oregano and pepper; brush on cut sides of bread top and bottom. On the bottom half, layer half of the meats, cheeses and green pepper. Repeat layers. Replace bread top. Wrap tightly in plastic wrap; refrigerate for up to 24 hours. **Yield: 10-12 servings.**

Make-Ahead Sloppy Joes

Alyne Fuller ✳ ODESSA, TEXAS

I frequently made big batches of these flavorful, filled buns when our six children were growing up. Having the zesty sandwiches in the freezer was such a time-saver on busy days. Now my kids make them for their families.

USES LESS FAT, SUGAR OR SALT. INCLUDES NUTRITION FACTS.

1	pound bulk pork sausage
1	pound ground beef
1	medium onion, chopped
14	to 16 sandwich buns, split
2	cans (8 ounces *each*) tomato sauce
2	tablespoons prepared mustard
1	teaspoon dried parsley flakes
1	teaspoon garlic powder
1	teaspoon salt
1/4	teaspoon pepper
1/4	teaspoon dried oregano

In a large skillet, brown sausage, beef and onion. Remove from the heat; drain. Remove the centers from the tops and bottoms of each bun. Tear removed bread into small pieces; add to skillet. Set buns aside.

Stir in remaining ingredients into sausage mixture. Spoon about 1/3 cupful onto the bottom of each bun; replace tops. Wrap individually in heavy-duty foil.

Bake at 350° for 20 minutes or until heated through or freeze for up to 3 months.

To use frozen sandwiches: Bake sandwiches at 350° for 35 minutes or until heated through. **Yield: 14-16 servings.**

NUTRITION FACTS: 1 sloppy joe equals 294 calories, 12 g fat (5 g saturated fat), 24 mg cholesterol, 672 mg sodium, 33 g carbohydrate, 2 g fiber, 14 g protein.

Make-Ahead Sloppy Joes

Sandwich for a Crowd

Sandwich for a Crowd

Helen Hougland ✳ SPRING HILL, KANSAS

My husband and I live on a 21-acre horse ranch and are pleased to invite friends to enjoy it with us. When entertaining, I rely on no-fuss, make-ahead entrees like this satisfying sandwich.

2	loaves (1 pound *each*) unsliced Italian bread
1	package (8 ounces) cream cheese, softened
1	cup (4 ounces) shredded cheddar cheese
3/4	cup sliced green onions
1/4	cup mayonnaise
1	tablespoon Worcestershire sauce
1	pound thinly sliced fully cooked ham
1	pound thinly sliced roast beef
12	to 14 thin slices dill pickle

Cut the bread in half lengthwise. Hollow out top and bottom of loaves, leaving a 1/2-in. shell (discard removed bread or save for another use).

In a large bowl, combine cheeses, onions, mayonnaise and Worcestershire sauce; spread over cut sides of bread. Layer ham and roast beef on bottom and top halves; place pickles on bottom halves. Gently press halves together.

Wrap in plastic wrap and refrigerate for at least 2 hours. Cut into 1-1/2-in. slices. **Yield: 12-14 servings.**

General Recipe Index

*INDICATES USES LESS FAT, SUGAR OR SALT. INCLUDES NUTRITION FACTS.

HAM (continued)
Salads
Sandwich for a Crowd, 107
Scrambled Egg Brunch Bread, 81
Super Italian Sub, 106
Super Sandwich, 42

HOT SANDWICHES (also see
Burgers; Open-Faced Sandwiches; Pocket
Sandwiches; Stromboli; Subs, Hoagies &
Heroes; Wraps)
Bacon 'n' Egg Sandwiches, 9
Bagel Melts, 90
Baked Brunch Sandwiches, 79
Breakfast in a Biscuit, 76
Breakfast Loaf, 76
Catfish Po'boys, 9
Chicken Apricot Bundles, 87
Citrus Fish Tacos, 84
Curry Cheddar Grill, 28
Dilly Chicken Sandwiches, 28
French Toast Sandwiches, 76
Fried Green Tomato Sandwiches, 25
Fry Bread Sandwiches, 86
Giant Sandwich, 100
Glazed Corned Beef Sandwiches, 97
Grilled Roast Beef Sandwiches, 22
Hacienda Hot Dogs, 89
Ham Wafflewiches, 78
Honey-Citrus Chicken Sandwiches, 28
Hot Colby Ham Sandwiches, 23
Huevos Rancheros, 79
Lasagna Sandwiches, 30
*Luau Chicken Sandwiches, 22
*Make-Ahead Sloppy Joes, 107
*Mom's Portable Beef, 98
Omelet Biscuit Cups, 75
Omelet Quesadilla, 77
Peppery Philly Steaks, 12
Pork and Corn Barbecue, 99
Raspberry Chicken Sandwiches, 27
Reuben Monte Cristos, 23
Reunion Steak Sandwiches, 20
Sausage Pepper Sandwiches, 21
Taco Sandwich, 26
Teriyaki Chicken Sandwiches, 25
Turkey Divan Croissants, 21
Ultimate Chicken Sandwiches, 20
Waffle Sandwiches, 74

LEMON & LIME
Citrus Chiffon Salad, 70
Honey-Citrus Chicken Sandwiches, 28
Lime Delight, 64

NUTS & PEANUT BUTTER
Apple-Nut Tossed Salad, 58
Apple-Strawberry Peanut Salad, 70
Apple-Walnut Turkey Sandwiches, 10
Cashew Turkey Pasta Salad, 6
Ham Pecan Pitas, 85
*Honey-Pecan Kiwi Salad, 57
Lunch Box Special, 34
Nutty Ham and Apple Sandwiches, 40
Peachy Pecan Salad, 58

Peanut Chicken Salad, 58
Walnut-Cheese Spinach Salad, 57

OPEN-FACED SANDWICHES
*Asparagus Chicken Sandwiches, 24
Bacon-Tomato Bagel Melts, 7
Brunch Pizza Squares, 74
Ham and Cheese Bagels, 93
Onion Beef Au Jus, 14
Spinach Egg Croissants, 81
Tropical Tuna Melts, 26

ORANGE
Citrus Chiffon Salad, 70
Citrus Fish Tacos, 84
Cran-Orange Turkey Bagel, 85
Cranberry Orange Vinaigrette, 15
Honey-Citrus Chicken Sandwiches, 28
*Sweet-Sour Citrus Salad, 12

PASTA & NOODLES
*Basil Pasta and Ham Salad, 70
Bow Tie Garden Pasta, 104
Cashew Turkey Pasta Salad, 6
Chicken Tortellini Salad, 66
Cool Cucumber Pasta, 97
*Fruited Pasta Salad, 100
German Hot Noodle Salad, 17
Hearty Pasta Salad, 12
*Oriental Pasta Salad, 69
Picnic Pasta Salad, 68
Spicy Ravioli Salad, 15
Three-Pepper Pasta Salad, 64
*Tortellini Caesar Salad, 11

PASTA & RICE SALADS
*Basil Pasta and Ham Salad, 70
Bow Tie Garden Pasta, 104
Cashew Turkey Pasta Salad, 6
Chicken Tortellini Salad, 66
Cool Cucumber Pasta, 97
*Fruited Pasta Salad, 100
German Hot Noodle Salad, 17
Hearty Pasta Salad, 12
*Mediterranean Medley Salad, 71
*Oriental Pasta Salad, 69
Picnic Pasta Salad, 68
Spicy Ravioli Salad, 15
Three-Pepper Pasta Salad, 64

PEPPERS
Fajita Pitas, 17
Pepper Lover's BLT, 36
Peppery Philly Steaks, 12
Sausage Pepper Calzones, 92
Sausage Pepper Sandwiches, 21
Three-Pepper Pasta Salad, 64

PINEAPPLE
Citrus Fish Tacos, 84
*Luau Chicken Sandwiches, 22
Tropical Tuna Melts, 26

POCKET SANDWICHES
Cold Sandwiches
Egg Salad Pitas, 91

Fresh Veggie Pockets, 93
Ham Pecan Pitas, 85
*Mediterranean Chicken Sandwiches,
   39
Hot Sandwiches
Apple Sausage Pitas, 74
Broccoli Ham Turnovers, 88
*Confetti Scrambled Egg Pockets, 80
Fajita Pitas, 17
Italian Chicken Pockets, 89
Meat Loaf Gyros, 87
Mother's Pasties, 91
Pork Pocket Pasties, 85
Sausage Pepper Calzones, 92
Smoked Sausage Pockets, 77

PORK (also see Bacon & Canadian
Bacon; Ham; Salami & Pepperoni; Sausage
& Hot Dogs)
Italian Pork Hoagies, 27
Mother's Pasties, 91
Oriental Pork Burgers, 11
Pork and Corn Barbecue, 99
Pork Salad Rolls, 87
Southwestern Pulled Pork, 13
Super Sandwich, 42
Zesty Breakfast Burritos, 75

POTATO SALADS
Caesar Chicken Potato Salad, 63
Cucumber Potato Salad, 66
German Potato Salad, 105
Golden Apple Potato Salad, 101
Hash Brown Potato Salad, 64
Irish Potato Salad, 65
*Roasted Potato Salad, 102

POTATOES & SWEET POTATOES
Caesar Chicken Potato Salad, 63
Cucumber Potato Salad, 66
German Potato Salad, 105
Golden Apple Potato Salad, 101
Hash Brown Potato Salad, 64
Irish Potato Salad, 65
*Roasted Potato Salad, 102
Sweet Potato Slaw, 68

SALAMI & PEPPERONI
Boston Subs, 105
Hot Pizza Subs, 25
Italian Subs, 36
Pizza Loaf, 30
Submarine Sandwich Salad, 50
Super Italian Sub, 106
Super Sandwich, 42

SAUSAGE & HOT DOGS
Apple Sausage Pitas, 74
Breakfast in a Biscuit, 76
Brunch Pizza Squares, 74
Hacienda Hot Dogs, 89
*Make-Ahead Sloppy Joes, 107
Pork Pocket Pasties, 85
Sausage Egg Subs, 80
Sausage Pepper Sandwiches, 21
Smoked Sausage Pockets, 77

Alphabetical Index
✶INDICATES USES LESS FAT, SUGAR OR SALT. INCLUDES NUTRITION FACTS.